The contents of this book regarding the accuracy of events, people and places depicted and permissions to use all previously published materials are the sole responsibility of the author who assumes all liability for the content of the book.

© 2020 Allan H. Topping

All rights reserved. Except for fair use educational purposes and short excerpts for editorial reviews in journals, magazines, or web sites, no part of this book shall be reproduced, stored in a retrieval system, or transmitted by any means without the written permission of the author and/or publisher.

International Standard Book Number 13: 978-1-60452-171-9
International Standard Book Number 10: 1-60452-171-6
Library of Congress Control Number: 2020948582

BluewaterPress LLC
2922 Bella Flore Ter
New Smyrna Beach, Florida 32168

http://www.bluewaterpress.com

Cover photo: courtesy of The Pan Am Historical Foundation

Wings of Freedom

Allan H. Topping

Table of Contents

Introduction	vii
Chapter 1 The Vietnam War	1
Chapter 2 Looking Through the Window	6
Chapter 3 Pan Am Employment	9
Chapter 4 Assignment Vietnam	17
Chapter 5 Cease-Fire Agreement Signed in Paris	29
Chapter 6 Tourism and Foreign Investment	32
Chapter 7 Trouble on the Horizon	36
Chapter 8 Operation Babylift	38
Chapter 9 The End Is Near	50
Chapter 10 Final Departure	61
Chapter 11 Final Flight Plan / Cleared for Takeoff	76
Chapter 12 A New Life Begins in Guam, USA	80
Chapter 13 Return to Vietnam 15 Years Later	85
Chapter 14 Last Employee Arrives In The US	92
Chapter 15 The Movie - Last Flight Out	95
Chapter 16 Saigon Station Closes	98
Chapter 17 Recollections of Former Pan Am Employees	100
About the Author	137

Introduction

I had the opportunity to live and work in South Vietnam for two and a half years. During that period, as the country Director, I handled the Pan Am operations in South Vietnam and Cambodia. In that role, I was the company's official representative. In addition to the operations, sales, services, and marketing assets of the job, I was engaged in public relations and government affairs. When I began my assignment in November of 1972, my main focus was our operations in Saigon. There was much to do. The war effort was winding down and it was necessary to initiate a number of staffing changes and costs reductions. Reducing our staff was difficult for me to justify because of the minimal level of salaries vis-a-vis the productivity benefits.

At that time we were operating twice weekly 747 services from Saigon to San Francisco via Manila, Guam, and Honolulu. We also worked an occasional all-cargo flight with Boeing 707 Freighter aircraft. The cargo service, carrying mail and cargo, operated in support of our US military contract. The routing included limited services through Danang. Located north of Saigon, Danang was South Vietnam's second largest city.

In addition to its global network of scheduled services, Pan Am on several occasions was involved in many rescue and humanitarian operations throughout the world. The airline was involved in the Berlin Airlift, the Cuban Airlift, rescue operations from Tehran, operational support for US forces in WW II, the Korean War, the Vietnam War and, more recently, the Gulf War. During the height of the Vietnam War, Pan Am's Vietnam flight operations represented the largest number of flights in the Pan Am system. The large number of flights operating in and out of South Vietnam were primarily the Rest and Relaxation Program (R & R) flights for military personnel serving in the war.

Because of the involvement, support, and dedication from numerous Pan Am departments, many Pan Am employees, and with the grace of God, we were able, on April 24, 1975, to successfully evacuate 463 American and Vietnamese civilians aboard a Boeing 747. Just six days after our departure, the North Vietnamese tanks rolled into downtown Saigon and the Vietnam war was finally over.

Our last flight, a dramatic and little-known event, was the basis for a television film which aired on the NBC-TV Network on May 22, 1990. The film, entitled Last Flight Out, featured James Earl Jones, Richard Crenna and Dr. Haing S. Ngor, the Academy Award winner for his role in The Killing Fields.

The film did not take on a political position nor do I plan to do so in this book. My primary motivation is to share another side of the Vietnam experience that was not featured in the movie nor on the network evening news back home. I will, therefore, share some additional events that occurred prior to, during and after our evacuation.

Perhaps the most profound lesson I learned during my Vietnam assignment was the fact that, when people are drawn together and faced with very real life-threatening and unknown situations, a unique bond develops between them regardless of ethnicity or beliefs. I am proud and deeply touched to say that, after more than forty-five years, the bond with my Vietnamese friends continues.

As the Pan Am Director in Saigon, it was up to me to make the final decision as to who would be aboard our last departure from South Vietnam. Pan Am senior management gave the final approval to evacuate all our employees and their "immediate" family members. There were sixty-two Vietnamese and two American employees at the time. The decisions that had to be made during that time were, without a doubt, the most difficult that I've ever had to make.

Dan Hood, a Pan Am pilot, arrived in Saigon three or four days prior to our final departure. His role in the film depicted a number of events related to the evacuation which were not entirely accurate. Dan was there solely to assist in getting some people out for a family in Seattle, Washington. He was successful in achieving that goal.

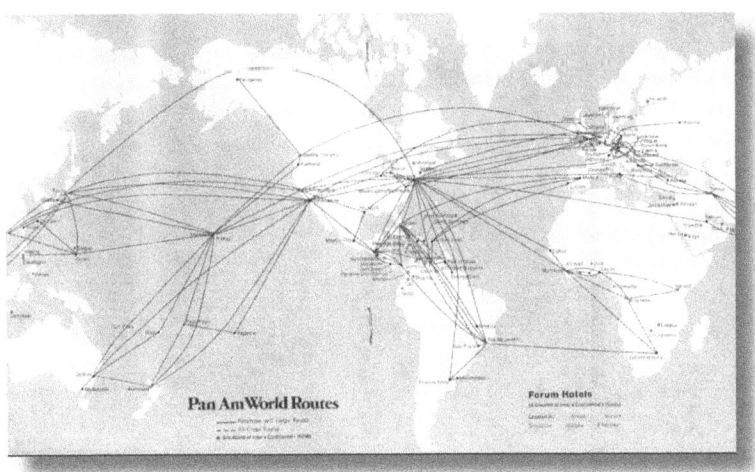

Pan Am was known for its pioneering in aviation and operated scheduled services to over one-hundred destinations on six continents. In a number of cases Pan Am was the only US carrier operating to several remote destinations, often times with once or twice-weekly services.

Chapter 1
The Vietnam War

Vietnam was ruled under French colonialism beginning in the Nineteenth Century. The Vietnam War started decades ago. Long before the United States became involved, Japanese forces had invaded Vietnam. After the Japanese were defeated in WW II, they withdrew their forces from Vietnam. Following the Japanese withdrawal, Bao Dai, the French educated Emperor, was in control; but Ho Chi Minh and his forces took over the northern city of Hanoi. This defeat paved the way for Ho Chi Minh to form a government similar to the Chinese and Soviet system of communism. Ho then declared a Democratic Republic of Vietnam (DRV), installing himself as president.

In the interim, the French continued to back Bao Dai and installed him to lead the newly formed state of Vietnam in the southern part of the country, in the city of Saigon. This took place in 1949. Ironically, both sides favored a unified country, but their differences precluded that objective. Ho Chi Minh desired a nation similar to other communist countries and Bao Dai wanted a system that was closer to economic and cultural ties with the West.

The northern and southern forces engaged in military battles until the battle of Dien Bien Phu in May 1954, which ended the French occupation after almost a century of French colonial rule. In July 1954, at a Geneva conference, a treaty was signed confirming the split of Vietnam along the 17th Parallel, resulting in a North and South Vietnam. In 1955 Emperor Bao was forced out by Ngo Dinh Diem who became president of the Republic of Vietnam. President Dwight Eisenhower pledged his support to Diem and South Vietnam. At that point in time the US modified its foreign policies to take a hardline approach to any allies of the Soviet Union. The Diem Administration, however, faced communist sympathizers in the South who were called Viet Cong (Vietnamese Communist). A major crackdown ensued resulting in tens of thousands of arrests followed by brutal tortures and executions. By 1957 the Viet Cong and other opponents to Diem were engaged in full blown firefights with the South Vietnamese Army.

In 1961 President John F. Kennedy dispatched a team to South Vietnam to assess the conditions on the ground. Their conclusion was the Domino Theory, which meant that, if one of the Southeast Asian nations fell into the hands of communism, several others in the region would probably follow. Based on the Domino Theory, and, in view of the current situation, Kennedy increased US aid to South Vietnam but did not commit to any large-scale military intervention. In 1962 the US did, however, increase its military troop size in South Vietnam to about nine thousand. This increase was significant when compared to eight-hundred troops in the 1950s.

In 1963 the situation in South Vietnam began to unravel on several fronts. A coup by some of Diem's own generals was successful in toppling Diem and his brother. This event occurred three weeks prior to Kennedy's assassination. As the instability in the region continued, Kennedy's successor, Lyndon Johnson with the support of Congress, Secretary of Defense, Robert

McNamara, decided to increase economic and military aid to South Vietnam.

In August 1964, the North Vietnamese torpedoed two US destroyers in the Gulf of Tonkin which triggered a major shift in the US involvement in the conflict. President Johnson received approval from Congress, passing the Gulf of Tonkin Resolution, giving Johnson expanded war making powers. The US began conducting massive bombing raids on North Vietnam under the code name, Rolling Thunder. These raids increased to include neighboring Laos, which contained other communist forces. With the support of the American public, Johnson continued to increase the number of combat troops in the war effort.

By November of 1967, with ongoing increases in troop strength, the American forces in Vietnam were rapidly approaching 500,000. By 1969 the US troop strength peaked to over 542,000. The increase in troops also produced an increase in casualties. At this point the US count in casualties was over 15,000 and almost 110,000 wounded. Eventually the war's toll reached more than 3.5 million dead.

South Vietnamese:
223,745 soldiers dead:
2 million civilians dead
North Vietnamese, Viet Cong:
(1954-1975): 1.1 million dead

Americans:
47,613 combat deaths;
10,800 other deaths;
2,029 missing

The beginning of the end of the Vietnam War began with the anti-war movement in the US and the termination of economic and military aid to South Vietnam.

Another turning point in the war was the Tet Offensive in 1968. The communist troops simultaneously attacked hundreds of urban areas in South Vietnam. One unit penetrated the US Embassy compound in Saigon killing five Americans. Most of the areas they invaded were recovered by allied forces except for the imperial city of Hue which they held for twenty-five days.

There were several massive anti-war demonstrations throughout the US. The largest demonstration took place in Washington D.C. in November 1969, when over 250,000 Americans held a peaceful march demanding the withdrawal of American troops from Vietnam. The anti-war movement was highly active on college campuses throughout the US. The killing of four students by National Guardsmen on the campus of Kent State University in Ohio became a symbol of the anti-war movement. As protests continued, two more students were killed by police at Jackson State University in Mississippi.

In 1968 President Nixon appointed Henry Kissinger to begin high level secret peace talks with the North Vietnamese in Paris. Initially the talks stalled, due to some of the demands of the North Vietnamese. Nevertheless the talks did resume and finally, in January 1973, a final peace agreement was reached, and the war was "over."

Unfortunately, it was not over. President Nguyen Van Thieu decided on a new strategy to offset the termination of American aid. He ordered the South Vietnamese army to basically pull out of all the northern provinces in the South and redeploy them to shore up the areas around Saigon. This move was an open invitation for the North Vietnamese army to start heading south unimpeded, and indeed they did. In fact, province after province fell without a shot fired. The North Vietnamese Army (NVA) was at least two years ahead of its master plan to conquer the South. Their southward march stalled about thirty miles from Saigon. The NVA stretched out for miles throughout South Vietnam and in dire need of replenishing their supplies. This delay of the inevitable provided the final window of escape for thousands of South Vietnamese and Americans. The war between the North and South, however, continued until April 30, 1975, when the North Vietnamese rolled into downtown Saigon and the city renamed Ho Chi Minh City.

In the end, the US spent $120 billon on the Vietnam War. Over sixty-thousand Americans died, millions of Vietnamese on both sides perished, and tens of thousands injured.

In 1994 President Clinton lifted the trade embargo against Vietnam and in 1995 a US Embassy opened in Hanoi. In 1997, two years later, Secretary of State Madeleine Albright opened a US consulate in Ho Chi Minh City and Vietnam opened a consulate in San Francisco.

Chapter 2
Looking Through the Window

It was in 1945, at the age of six when I got my first look at a Pan Am aircraft. I do not recall too many of the details other than the fact that the plane looked huge! I was probably wondering how something so large could fly and stay up in the air. My nine-year old sister, Yvonne, my Mother, Gwendolyn, and I were preparing to leave for Miami from Kingston, Jamaica. The three of us were leaving Jamaica to join my Father, Allan, in Brooklyn, New York. He left Jamaica in 1944 and immigrated to the U.S by way of a sponsorship from an engineer in Boston, MA. I remember him as Mr. Dutton. He would spend part of the winter in Montego Bay at the Ethel Hart Hotel. My Father worked at the hotel as the all-around, multi-tasking handyman. He was the chauffeur, plumber, electrician, and waiter. I am certain that the engineer was impressed with the qualities he saw in my Father, took a liking to him, and decided to sponsor him.

The sponsorship requirement called for my Father to work for the Duttons in the United States for one year. At the end of the year, he had the option of staying on with the Duttons or venturing out on his own. He decided on the latter choice and sponsored my Mother, sister, and me so we could join him in the United States.

The long-awaited departure day finally arrived. We had been separated for a year. Now my Mother, sister and I were about to board a huge aircraft and fly off to a land that seemed so far away. I was excited. Perhaps it was at this moment that I became interested in travel and geography.

Once we boarded the plane, I sat by the window and immediately began watching and waiting for us to take off. I kept wondering how it was going to happen. The plane seemed so big and there seemed to be so many people onboard. As I watched all of the luggage being loaded, I wondered how we could possibly get off the ground! In all my excitement, I was oblivious to what feelings my mother and sister had about all of this drama, but I did learn years later that my mother was terrified and, because of that experience, she vowed to never fly again. She never did.

Suddenly the propellers began to turn, belching out blue smoke and flickering flames. Then the cabin began to vibrate. Was this normal? I guessed that it was because everyone stayed calmly seated. With all the propellers turning, we slowly began to move away from the terminal. The noise and vibration continued. It was getting exciting! I pressed my nose against the window. Once we taxied to the end of the runway, we held for a short period of time and then suddenly it was full throttle, excessive vibration and we began to rumble down the runway for take-off. A few seconds later we were in the air and I was simply amazed as the scene below gradually got smaller.

Almost immediately, we were over the blue waters of the Caribbean. At some point along the way we encountered some turbulence. I was so fascinated with the view out the window that I probably never looked away during the entire flight from Kingston, via Havana, Cuba to Miami, Florida. I don't think I noticed anything that was going on inside the cabin.

Little did I know at the time that, some thirty years later, I would again be glued to the window on another Pan Am flight; but for an entirely different reason. This time it would be aboard a Pan Am Boeing 747 with a very different flight plan, in an overloaded cabin with frightened, desperate Vietnamese whose lives would never be the same again.

Chapter 3
Pan Am Employment

My first exposure to the travel industry began in 1961. I worked as a Transportation Specialist for the Institute of International Education (IIE). The Institute was located at One East 67th Street on the corner of 5th Avenue in New York City. It was formerly a Vanderbilt Mansion converted into a very elegant three-story office building. A beautiful, winding marble staircase was the first thing one would see when entering through the main door. Located just across the street from Central Park, the location could not have been more ideal. Lunch in the park during the spring and summer was wonderful. Two years later the Institute moved to 809 UN Plaza, across the street from the United Nations Building. The Institute was a nonprofit organization that served as a clearing house for processing thousands of foreign exchange students. The students were recipients of grants provided by various foundations and the US State Department. We worked with two primary travel agents and directly with the airlines making the transportation arrangements from their home countries to their final destination in the US. A number of the grantees came from remote locations throughout the world, places like South Vietnam, Laos, Cambodia, Thailand, India, Asia, and a number of countries on the African Continent. It was at that time that I became familiar with the globe, as I referred to it on a daily basis. It was absolutely an essential part of our office reference material and played a key role in planning the students' itineraries. Truthfully, I had no idea where some of those foreign countries and cities were located. The grants that were awarded provided college and university placements throughout the US.

As a Transportation Specialist, I was responsible for making the travel arrangements for a significant number of foreign students from their home country to universities and colleges throughout the United States. That was when I began to develop a special interest in international cultures. Some of the students would visit our New York office on their way to their final US destination. It was so interesting when the foreign students would visit our office for the first time, dressed in their native apparel. Quite often, after their first semester, they would visit us again, and we would do a double take, because they would be wearing the current fashion trend. I always enjoyed those moments; it was so interesting to see how quickly they would become "Americanized" as their native garb was, at least for the time being, put aside.

On a number of occasions it was often necessary to meet a student arriving at John F. Kennedy International Airport (JFK). I would help them through government arrival formalities and transport them to a hotel in the city. Although those encounters were brief, they did provide an opportunity to learn a few things about their home country, their culture, and their first impressions of the US. The opportunity to meet and communicate with such a wide variety of people from so many foreign countries was most interesting to me. I often thought that it was such a wonderful opportunity for those students to live and get an education at some of the finest learning institutions in the United States. Their entire education was fully paid for through the student grantee program. The more I learned about their home countries the more I wanted to know what life was like in their homeland. My curiosity started to percolate, and I began to develop a desire to travel and visit some of those places.

During this time, and because of my exposure to a diverse group of students from various foreign nations, my geographical knowledge of the United States and the world reached a notable level. So much so that the urge to travel began to be part of my daily thoughts, hopes and dreams. Little did I know at the time that, in the not-too-distant future, those aspirations would be realized far beyond my wildest expectations.

After five years at the Institute I had an offer to join the United Airlines Passenger Service team at JFK. During the interview I was told that public contact employees at United were not allowed to have a mustache or a beard and was asked if I would be willing to shave off my mustache. I said, "Of course I will!" As I look around today, I can only say, "My, how the times have changed!" It's now not just about hair, but how about those tattoos and body jewelry? I still prefer the mustache instead of some piece of jewelry hanging from my lower lip or a head of hair that looks like a weapon.

I enjoyed the challenges that came with the duties of the Passenger Services Agent. What made the job unique and challenging was the fact that every day was different. There were different passengers, different flight crews, different weather conditions, and a variety of operational issues. In other words, there was never a dull moment. Some of the most challenging situations occurred when flights diverted to alternate airports due to local weather conditions. This would sometimes result in extremely long delays spilling over into the next couple of days affecting passengers from the West Coast to the East Coast and everywhere in between.

One of the most bizarre incidents I experienced as a Passenger Service Agent happened one Friday evening. The 6:00 p.m. nonstop flight to Chicago's O'Hare's Airport was overbooked. Passengers without confirmed reservations were placed on a standby list. It was a prime departure time. As I was writing the ticket for a passenger, he suddenly dropped to the floor, right in front of me, at the ticket counter. My supervisor rushed over and tried mouth-to-mouth resuscitation and chest pumps, but there was no response. By the time the paramedics arrived, it was too late. He had passed. What happened next was quite amazing. The passenger next in line asked me, "What are the chances of getting on the 6'clock flight to Chicago?" I informed him that the flight was full, and I would add him to the standby list. He then asked, as he pointed to the man stretched out on the floor, "What flight was he on? He's not going anywhere!" I just stopped and stared at him in disbelief. At that moment I was in some stage of shock and sadness over what had happened, just five or ten minutes earlier. When I gained some level of composure, I did add him to the standby list. To this day I don't recall if he ever made the flight.

One day I showed up for work wearing a suit because my uniform was not ready at the dry cleaners. The Station Manager approached me asking what happened to my uniform. He took me aside and told me that I looked great in the suit and wanted to know if I would be interested in taking part in an experimental passenger service sales project. It would be a temporary position and my new title would be Service Director.

The Service Director would be the manager of all aspects of the pre-boarding procedures and pre-departure needs of all of the nonstop flights to the West Coast. At the time United Airlines had three daily non-stops to Los Angeles, two daily non-stops to San Francisco and one to Seattle. At the departure gate the Service Director would make the pre-boarding and boarding announcements, check with the flight attendants to ensure that all of their required supplies where onboard, and that the cabin was properly cleaned and ready for boarding.

At the departure gate podium, the key role of the Service Director was to check all the tickets pulled by the gate agent and to look for tickets that did not have a return flight reservation. The next step was to approach the passenger and offer to book his return flight back to New York on United right there on the spot. The passengers were most impressed with this service. By having this ability to reserve return flights in this manner we were minimizing the possibility of the passenger deciding to book their return flight on United's competitor.

As we began tracking the data of the last-minute departure gate bookings, the revenue figures were getting the attention of management. Due to the success of this program, the Service Director position was expanded to the West Coast; so now we had this incremental revenue producer locked in on both sides of the country.

The position also included one more important service. Working with our Special Services Team, we would also help in meeting and greeting VIP's. Working in that role, I had the opportunity to meet a number of celebrities, various executives, and many others of the famous and not so famous. To name a few, I met and assisted Bob Hope, Mohammed Ali, Bill Cosby, Simon & Garfunkel, Ed McMahon, Ray Charles, Dr. Martin Luther King, Barbara Walters, and many CEO's.

Since United was the primary carrier of professional sports teams, I also had the opportunity to meet a number of players from the National Football League and Major League Baseball. I will always remember one particular sports charter flight that I met on arrival at JFK. As the airplane came to a stop at the gate and I opened the cabin door, standing there with a bottle of Johnny Walker Black in one hand, and his arms wrapped around a United Airlines flight attendant in the other, was a New York Jets player. Everyone was all smiles. It must have been some kind of a flight. The Jets had just returned on the red eye from California after losing to the Oakland Raiders.

I have a binder with several letters of commendation as a result of providing various services to so many VIP passengers. A typical service was to meet and greet a VIP passenger at curbside as they stepped out of their limo. Their curbside baggage check-in was expedited and I would escort them to the Red Carpet Room where they could relax and enjoy their favorite beverage prior to boarding. If necessary, I would also escort them to the gate area and into the cabin to their first class seat.

During my role as a Service Director I also had an opportunity to meet a number of Pan Am executives who frequently flew to the West Coast on United Airlines. Some of the Pan Am executives were frequent flyers on United and I began to develop a professional relationship with a number of them. At that time Pan Am did not have domestic routes. I guess they were impressed with how I performed my job, because one day the Interline Sales Manager for the New York Region said to me, "If you ever decide to leave United, please give me a call." Her name was Connie Citrano.

One afternoon I decided to visit the Pan Am Worldport Terminal at JFK. When I entered the terminal, I was struck by the destinations listed on the electronic departure board: London, Paris, Rome, Frankfurt, Bombay, etc. It was as if the terminal was the launching pad for global air travel. As I would find out later, it was indeed Pan Am's world.

When I returned to the United Airlines terminal that afternoon, I looked at the departure board listing Cleveland, Los Angeles, Chicago, Denver, and our other US destinations. They just did not have the same ring to them. Fine cites but just not the same.

I enjoyed working for United, but after five years at the airport I felt a need to move into the sales and marketing area. I had learned just about everything there was to know about airport customer services. I approached my boss about the possibility of transferring to the United Sales Department downtown and to see if there were any Sales Representative positions available. He made a couple of phone calls to the sales office and an interview was arranged. I thought that my first interview with the New York Sales Manager went well; however, I was told there were no openings at that time.

I decided to call Connie Citrano at Pan Am. She arranged an interview for me with her and the Vice President for North America, George Camaan. The interview went very well. A sales representative position was available and the job was mine, should I decide to leave United. They told me to think it over and let them know whether I would accept their offer. This was an exciting and difficult moment for me. I always thought of Pan Am as the premier carrier. United was also an outstanding airline, and at that time had the world's largest fleet of aircraft.

I thought about the times I escorted VIP's arriving at JFK to the Pan Am Worldport Terminal so they could continue on to an international destination. At those times I was convinced that one day my goal would be to visit as many of those destinations as possible.

So this was my dilemma. I advised my boss at United that Pan Am had offered me the sales representative position and I had to let them know if I would accept the offer. He told me that United wanted me to stay, because I had done such an outstanding job, and that they would really hate to lose me. He talked me into letting him make a couple of phone calls and suggested I go downtown one more time to see if there were any openings in the Sales Department. I went for the second interview and, sure enough, suddenly there was a sales rep opening with United Airlines. So now what would I do? That difficult decision was made, and I decided to take the Pan Am offer. I was hired by Pan Am on June 2, 1969.

It is a decision that I will never regret. The Pan Am experience provided unlimited travel opportunities for my family and me. We could travel the world; as the saying goes, "Those faraway places with the strange sounding names." We visited a few. There were a number of special characteristics about the Pan Am company. We were a family. Working together, either on the job or via telex (now known as email) to co-workers at some exotic location around the globe, special relationships formed. One of the most special moments for me was when I climbed aboard a 747 to head back home to the good old USA. Regardless of where I happened to be in the world, while waiting in the departure gate area and seeing the Pan Am logo and the American flag on that tall tail, it was always a special moment when the plane pulled up to the gate. Once onboard, I knew I was back home in the US. I recall the time when I was on a station evaluation assignment in India and Turkey for three weeks. It was a difficult three weeks on the road. When the assignment was completed, I was waiting at the departure gate for my flight. As I watched the airplane approach the gate, I saw the familiar Pan Am logo and I thought, "Home, sweet home, here I come." Unless you have had the experience of boarding a Pan Am airplane thousands of miles away from the United States, you'll never know how special that feeling is. It was a feeling of more than just welcome aboard, it was also a special feeling of being welcomed home by a terrific team of Pan Am crew members.

Chapter 4
Assignment Vietnam

During the course of the orientation I was most impressed with the history of Pan Am. The airline was a true pioneer in commercial international aviation.

After about four to six weeks of orientation and an accelerated management training program, I was told I would be transferred to a Pan Am sales office in the United States. As the new kid on the block, I expected to be assigned to an off-line city. Off-line cities are locations where the airline does not operate and you are expected to generate revenue, via airline partners and travel agents, that would feed passengers into our major New York hub and all West Coast departures to Asia. This sales approach was a challenge simply because there was no way to board a Pan Am flight in an off-line city. In an off-line city, it would be necessary to create incentive programs to get travel agents to book passengers on Pan Am, via an intermediate stop on another airline. This was back in the day when travel agents were responsible for booking more than 50% of an airline's revenue. Those were indeed the good old days of travel. But today, due to the internet, travel agents are becoming the dinosaur of the industry. Now there are many websites available where travelers can easily make their own airline, hotel, car rental, and sightseeing tour reservations. In fact, today passengers can even print out their boarding passes from their home computer. That was unheard of in those days.

After a couple of weeks of orientation and management training, I received word that I was going to be a sales rep in the Northern California Sales Office and that I could begin planning my move to San Francisco. I was asked, "Is that okay with you, Al?" Once I started breathing again, I replied, "Are you kidding me? That's wonderful!" It was like a dream coming to life.

During my five years with United Airlines I made several trips to San Francisco. I'll always remember the view on my very first trip (looking out the window again). As we approached the airport, the fog was rolling in, the hills along the peninsula coastal areas were so picturesque; it was simply a beautiful sight. I can recall saying to myself, "Gee, someday I would love to live here." All of those thoughts would be flowing through my mind during final approach to San Francisco International Airport.

Living in the Bay Area was so different from the hustle and bustle of the East Coast. One of the first things I noticed was that everyone seemed to be more friendly. One could meet a total stranger on the street or on a fully loaded cable car; they would say hello and sometimes strike up a conversation. As I got to know people, I found that a large percentage of the people in the Bay Area were actually from the East Coast. Was it something in the water that fired up the warm and friendly attitude? After a five-day road trip across the US in a fully loaded Volkswagen Beetle, I moved into a hillside apartment in Sausalito. That location offered spectacular views of the City by the Bay and the Golden Gate Bridge.

A new beginning in the Bay Area was really the best of both worlds. The morning commute to the City on the Sausalito Ferry was the best way to get to work. There was no rush-hour traffic to deal with; I just sat back with a cup of coffee and opened the San Francisco Chronicle to catch up with the news of the day as we sailed passed the infamous Alcatraz Island prison. A short twenty-five minutes later the ferry docked at the Ferry Building in San Francisco and from there I had a short walk to the office at Number One California Street.

After a couple of years as a sales rep I was offered the job as Manager of Telephone Sales in the reservations office. It was a challenging and important position. The Reservations Sale Agent was often the first contact a customer had with the company. If professional and courteous service were not provided when handling a sales call, we could have easily lost a customer to the competition. This was an issue I constantly emphasized to our sales agents.

During the fourth quarter of 1972 Pan Am announced a company-wide reorganization and major changes were underway. A number of positions were eliminated and/or merged. Country directors were selected in the field divisions.

When I joined Pan Am, one of my long-term goals was to become a Pan Am station manager. I would always make that known during my annual performance reviews. Bill Cowden was the Director of Sales for the Northern California Region in San Francisco at that time. One day, he invited me into his office. I'll never forget that meeting. He popped the question, "Are you still interested in becoming a station manager?" "Of course, absolutely," I replied. Bill then informed me that he had a position coming up in the Pacific Division and wanted to know if I would be interested.

Bill Cowden said he was reassigned to Hong Kong and that I would be reporting to him. At this point I'm wondering, "Could this be Hawaii, (not a chance), Hong Kong, Singapore, Thailand, or perhaps Australia or the Philippines?" Bill told me that I would be the country director and the official Pan Am representative. "Terrific," I said, "What country is it?" He said,

"You would be the Director for our operations in South Vietnam and Cambodia and based in Saigon." My immediate response was, "Seriously? No thanks, Bill." Leaving the Bay Area to live in a war zone did not appeal to me at all. He tried to encourage me and told me I didn't have to decide at that moment. He wanted me to take a couple of days to think about it. "After all," he said, "the Paris peace talks are moving along on a positive track. The negotiations are ongoing and there may be a cease-fire agreement soon. While you are thinking about it, perhaps you should take a few days off, get on a plane and take a trip to Saigon. Plan on spending a few days there, meet the Pan Am staff, have a look around and then make a decision." I thought about it overnight and decided that I would make the trip. So, off I went to Saigon, South Vietnam via PA Flight #841.

It's a long trip from San Francisco to Saigon; crossing the Central Pacific with intermediate stops in Honolulu, Guam, and Manila before arriving. At a certain point during the seven-hour flight between Hawaii and Guam, the flight crosses the International Date Line which means if you left San Francisco on Tuesday evening, you arrive in Guam about 4:00 a.m. on Thursday morning. The flight then took off for Manila, then on to the final leg of the trip to Saigon.

After leaving Manila, I was getting curious and somewhat excited about actually flying into South Vietnam. Again, I'm looking out the window and I see that we are approaching the coastline of South Vietnam, the Vietnam that was always mentioned on the evening news about the protracted war. Now I was wondering if I would see any signs of war from the airplane window. As our flight continued toward Saigon, I did see some fighter jets and C-130 type aircraft flying in various directions below us. I also saw what appeared to be bomb craters scattered throughout the countryside. I noticed that we were making a very unusual approach into Tan Son Nhut Airport. Our approach on that particular day involved a huge circle on the outskirts of Saigon and continued descending into a corkscrew type of pattern, then leveling off into a final approach for landing. I assumed that this was probably a typical approach pattern used to avoid being hit by possible ground fire.

We taxied to our parking spot on the tarmac, the cabin door was opened, and a wave of heat greeted me, the likes of which I had never before experienced. It was extremely hot and humid, like walking into a sauna or sticking your head into an oven. At the bottom of the steps, my predecessor-to-be, Bob McElhatton, greeted me. He was waiting there with the company car and driver. Thankfully, the car had air conditioning. We left the aircraft and headed for the immigration and customs building to go through the government clearance formalities. Once inside the facility, I said to myself, "Welcome to the Third World!" The old wooden floors were very dirty, slow-turning ceiling fans were the only source of air conditioning, and the area for processing passengers was sorely inadequate.

The ride from the airport to the hotel in Saigon was overwhelming. The traffic was a sight to behold. The primary mode of transportation in Saigon was the Honda motorbike, commonly called cyclos. They were noisy and most of them produced an unusual amount of smoke from their faulty exhaust systems. As we continued our way to the hotel, I was amazed at the sight of four or five people riding on one motorbike. Some people would have a significant load of products on their motorbike, which they were taking to market or perhaps selling on a street corner. Some of the loads I saw that day included chickens and bundles of various vegetables slung over half the back seat. Interspersed throughout the traffic were three-wheel cyclo-taxis for hire. One of the more beautiful sights, mixed in with all the traffic, was the Vietnamese women wearing their traditional dress, the Ao Dai (pronounced as "ow zai"), as they sat side saddle on the motorbike with their dresses flowing in the breeze.

The arrival and check-in at the Regency Palace on Nguyen Hue Street was routine. There was nothing special in the lobby; only the usual furnishings that were typical in any hotel. There were, however, a couple of guys in the lobby who were wandering around, puffing on cigarettes, and giving me a curious look. I surmised that they were probably local police officers, in plain clothes, keeping an eye on the foreigners checking in and out of the hotel.

My hotel room was small, and the mattress was extra firm and not too comfortable. On the first evening in Saigon we had dinner at the hotel's rooftop restaurant. The terrain surrounding Saigon is flat and I could see for miles, all the way to the horizon. The rooftop view was spectacular. That evening, the reality of war made its first appearance to me. Off in the distance were flashes of fire, coupled with distinctive booms— the sound of bombs exploding. I said to Bob. "If that is what I think it is, I hope they're on our side!" He explained that it was pretty much a nightly occurrence, as the South Vietnamese were hitting suspected enemy targets. The practice had been going on for years. I wondered how many people died or were wounded by the indiscriminate dropping of bombs in the countryside of South Vietnam. A few days later my wondering became a reality. I saw the results of those bombings; mostly women, carrying or walking with their wounded children. Some of their babies were horribly scarred for life with severe burns on their faces and other parts of their little bodies. They were seen throughout the city. As I walked along, I was often approached by these mothers, begging for money. It was troubling and very sad. Some cases were so horrific that I could only look for a second or two. I had a difficult time making eye contact with them.

The hotel rooftop restaurant was not the only game in town. There were many cafes where one could enjoy any type of Vietnamese cuisine. If someone were looking for fine carpeting and candlelight dining, Saigon was not the place. But if one were looking for delicious and inexpensive food, sidewalk dining was the best choice. Sitting on small stools and eating alongside the locals was quite the experience. Sidewalk eating spots were everywhere. The locals frequented the majority of these eateries. But for the tourist that was looking to experience the local flavor of Saigon, they would not be disappointed in the delicious, inexpensive, and very satisfying meal found at a sidewalk cafe. Due to decades of the French influence in Vietnam, there were a number of good French restaurants as well.

During my one-week stay in Saigon I had an opportunity to tour all of our facilities and meet with all of our employees. Bob also arranged a reception so that I could meet some of the members of the business and diplomatic community. The reception was held at the Pan Am Director's residence. As I entered the residence for the first time, I was struck by the charm and structure of the classic old French villa. It had eighteen-foot-high ceilings, with ceiling fans and tall windows that were open to the warm, humid climate outside. There was no central air conditioning, only turning ceiling fans and open windows all around the room that provided cross ventilation. The only air-conditioned rooms were the master and guest bedrooms. Window air conditioner units were installed in those room and supplied comfortable and adequate cooling.

From a security standpoint the location of the residence was ideal. Directly across the street was the residential compound of the Vice President of South Vietnam. The walled compound had fully armed South Vietnamese soldiers overlooking the neighborhood from their lookout towers. Helicopters were in and out of the compound throughout the day and sometimes into the night. Next to the Vice President's residence was a US Embassy personnel compound, the residence for US diplomats and their families. Our next-door neighbor on one side was the President of Air Vietnam and on the other side was the home of the general manager for Citi Bank—not a bad neighborhood. The name of the street was Tu Xuon (too soon), known as the Quiet Street. So this would be home, should I decide to accept the assignment.

After spending a week in Saigon and meeting the Pan Am employees and those in the business and diplomatic community, it was time to make the long trip back to San Francisco. I knew that it was now decision time. I had lots of time to think about how my life would be affected if I decided to take the assignment. I was happy living in the Bay Area. I would miss those weekend trips to places like Lake Tahoe, the wine country in Sonoma and Napa Valley, the Gold Country and spending the night in Jackson, or heading down the Coast to Pebble Beach, Big Sur and the Monterrey Bay area. Surely, I would miss all of that and more.

More importantly, in North Carolina, was another part of my life that caused me pause in my decision-making process. My two children from an earlier marriage, Todd and Germaine lived in North Carolina with their mother. At the time Todd was six and Germaine was nine. From California I could get to them rather quickly, as it was only a four and a half-hour flight to North Carolina. Relocating almost 20,000 miles away was indeed a cause for concern. Being so far away made it seem like it would take days to get to North Carolina. This personal family matter added to the clutter of issues gathering in my mind. So much to think about, so little time.

There would be another important part of my California living that I would dearly miss. I would be flying off to Vietnam without Jan. Jan and I had been dating for nearly two years and we had a close and wonderful relationship. Since the relocation was happening so quickly, we decided that I would go ahead with the move, get acclimated to my new assignment, and then decide what to do about our relationship. The decision emerged rather quickly; three months later I returned to California and we were married on March 3, 1973 in a chapel on a hillside in beautiful Sausalito. We honeymooned in Hawaii, then went straight to Saigon to begin our life together.

During my first few weeks living and working in South Vietnam, I was looking forward to the challenges of managing an operation in a war zone. There was no training; it was simply a matter of my predecessor passing me the baton. We were fortunate in that all of our customer contact Vietnamese employees were bilingual, knowledgeable, and dedicated. They loved their job. For our Vietnamese employees, working for Pan Am represented what was a prestigious position in the eyes of the local community. For them, it was the equivalent of working for the US Government. Normally, working for the US Government overseas represented a positive image and a certain level of prestige for local employees. Just a short two and a half years later, however, US companies and their employees were looked upon in a totally different light.

Unfortunately, one of my first administrative actions was to reduce our operating expenses for the Saigon operation. This was extremely difficult for me because local salaries were incomparable to wages in the United States. Furthermore, the highly productive performance the employees provided on a day-to-day basis far outweighed the cost. Nevertheless, whenever cost cutting is on the agenda, reduction in headcount is usually the first item to be addressed. Those actions were necessary because of the reduction in flight operations. We were now operating only twice weekly 747 services and limited 707 cargo services into Danang and Saigon. The cargo flights were operated per our Military Airlift Command (MAC) contracts for carrying mail and cargo to our troops and US government civilian employees serving in South Vietnam.

Living in South Vietnam had no resemblance to what I expected. Being the news junkie that I am, rarely did I miss the CBS Evening News with Walter Cronkite and/or Huntley-Brinkley Report on NBC. Those nightly telecasts painted an entirely different picture than what I experienced there on the ground. The nightly news reports usually focused on the daily casualty counts for both sides. Most reports would conclude with what became a routine comment, "American casualties were light." We may never know the true casualty count, but for now we know that it was over 58,000. The combined casualties for both sides exceeded one million.

The day-to-day life was, in many ways, similar to living in any large city. Lots of shops, hustle and bustle in the streets, and extreme noise due to the enormous number of motorbikes constantly moving in all directions. There was no such thing as emissions control for the vast number of motorbikes nor, for that matter, any type of vehicle—making the level of pollution unbearable at times. Many locals wore masks in an effort to minimize inhaling the constant level of pollution. The motorbikes, which basically served as the family car, was, without a doubt, the most popular mode of transportation. Due to the high volume and usage of the motorbikes, a repair service industry was born. On any given street corner there would be a couple of teenage boys who could fix just about anything broken on a motorbike. If they did not have a part needed to repair a motorbike, they would simply make something up. Their ingenuity was amazing.

The Saigon assignment provided me an opportunity to check off an item on my bucket list. For many years, my dream was to host a late-night TV show or be a disc jockey on a local radio station. In Saigon there was a radio station that was part of the Armed Forces Radio & TV Network (ARFTS). It was the only English-speaking station in town. If you had a shortwave radio you could pick up several stations around the world. I bought a shortwave radio and it became a vital part of my communications network. When the situation in South Vietnam began to unravel, I was able to tune in to the British Broadcasting Corporation (BBC). They supplied important information about the troop movement of the North Vietnamese Army. One day I decided to stop by the ARFTS station to meet the manager. I asked him if it would be possible for me to volunteer to host a one-hour weekly program; I would play easy listening type of music. He said, "Not a problem, you're on." I was somewhat shocked that my offer was so easily accepted.

I began to do a one-hour live broadcast on Saturday evenings beginning at six o'clock. The program was called, Al Topping with the Good Vibrations. I had absolutely zero experience in

Jan and me in Sausalito, CA prior to my departure for the Saigon assignment, October 1972. (photo authors collection)

broadcasting. Suddenly, I was going to do a live radio show in Saigon, South Vietnam. Our primary listening audience consisted of the US troops that were in country, the diplomatic community, foreign business community, and the Vietnamese who were trying to improve their English language skills. It was also like having a Pan Am ad on air without ever mentioning the name of Pan Am. The music consisted of well-known artists from the 60's and 70's and each week I would feature a different album. The Sinatra album, called The Main Event, and Elvis, Judy Collins, Chicago, Harry Belafonte, and The Beatles were all featured on the radio show. I still have some of the tapes from the show. On my last broadcast, which aired around the end of March, the final song I played was a classic by Peter, Paul & Mary called, I'm Leaving on A Jet Plane.

Chapter 5
Cease-Fire Agreement Signed in Paris

When I began my assignment in Saigon in November 1972, there was an abundance of optimism in the air that the peace talks in Paris were moving in a positive direction and that a ceasefire agreement was finally within reach. The talks actually began in 1965. Serious negotiations, however, did not actually begin until 1968. Along the way there were deadlocks on various issues impeding the process. A classic example of this was the dispute about the seating arrangements and the shape of the table around which the talks would take place. There were prolonged discussions to resolve the table issue.

Officially, the Paris Peace Accords of 1973 were designed and intended to establish peace in Vietnam and finally put an end to the Vietnam War. The official title of the agreement was, "The Agreement on Ending the War and Restoring Peace in Vietnam." In North Vietnam, this agreement called for celebration, because they considered it a victory. In South Vietnam, however, there was no celebration. The South Vietnamese Government was skeptical from the beginning and believed that the agreement would only temporarily lead to peace. As it turned out, in the end the South Vietnamese were correct. In the United States, President Nixon and Secretary of State, Henry Kissinger, received praise from the media. They labeled it "peace with honor."

Negotiations with Hanoi included talks about the implementation of an aid program, as well as the establishment of diplomatic relations between the United States and North Vietnam. An integral piece of the agreement included the establishment of the International Commission for Control and Supervision (ICCS). Their primary role during the postwar era was to monitor the ceasefire for all the parties.

Finally, the protracted war was over. There would be no more killing and there would be peace at last. By the end of March of 1973, the last American combat troops left South Vietnam. I'll never forget the day when the last of the American troops were boarding the chartered flights at Tan Son Nhut Airport and heading back to the US. There was a North Vietnamese soldier in a pith helmet, with a clipboard and a clicker, counting the US troops as they boarded the airplane. At one point, during the height of the war, the US Embassy in South Vietnam was the largest in the world. During that peak period, including the Rest and Relaxation (R&R) flights and scheduled flights, the Pan Am operation in South Vietnam was the largest in the worldwide Pan Am system. After all of that massive involvement in the war it came down to a clipboard and a clicker, counting the last of the US troops as they boarded airplanes heading back to the USA. I thought it was such a surreal sight. After all the battles, all the casualties, and all the devastation; this one person was making sure that all the US troops were finally leaving Vietnam. A limited number of US Marines would remain in order to protect the US facilities, such as the American Embassy. A limited number of military advisors would also remain to continue their role working with the South Vietnamese Army.

Although the South Vietnamese government signed onto the Peace Accords, they viewed it as a significant disadvantage for their future security. They felt that the Peace Accords were designed favorably for the North Vietnamese and would eventually result in the collapse of South Vietnam. In the end, they were absolutely correct. The Agreement was structured to allow the North to maintain some of their troops in certain provinces in the South.

Chapter 6
Tourism and Foreign Investment

The war that seemed would never end was finally over. Peace at last. The South Vietnamese Government's priority immediately shifted into commercial development. One of the programs near the top of the agenda was tourism. South Vietnam is blessed with an abundance of beautiful, natural beaches with seemingly endless stretches of white sand and crystal-clear water. Almost at once the government selected the former vice president of Air Vietnam to be the Minister of Tourism.

On a beautiful bright, sunshiny day several representatives from multinational companies, boarded helicopters and flew to two offshore islands in the South China Sea. We visited Con Son Island and the Island of Phu Cuoc. The inescapable Con Son Island was well known for the so-called tiger cages. The prison cages were constructed and used by the French for torture and extreme brutality.

The French influence in Vietnam had been born decades before. Most Vietnamese were bilingual, fluent in French and Vietnamese. There were a number of French restaurants in Saigon. The Circle Sportiff Club, located in the heart of the city, was patronized by foreigners and Vietnamese. On any given day, the bikini-clad Eurasians, as well as Vietnamese women, were found lounging by the pool or playing tennis.

The Saigon Golf and Country Club was next to Tan Son Nhut International Airport, a very popular facility for members of the foreign community; in fact, that was where I first took up the game of golf. Playing golf in Saigon was about the same as walking through an outdoor sauna. It was always hot and extremely humid. There were no golf carts; golfers had to walk. The only saving grace was that there was a caddy (usually a young woman) for every golfer. To this day I continue to be amazed at how the caddies could walk for eighteen holes, in the intense heat and humidity, carrying a golf bag filled with clubs. Incredibly, it was not unusual to have one caddy carrying two sets of golf clubs; one set slung over each shoulder. To protect them from the sun, their clothing would cover them from head to toe; the uniform was a long-sleeved pink jacket and black, silky pants down to their ankles. Most of the time, they wore no shoes. I soon found out that, whenever a player's ball ended up in the rough, it would always end up sitting nicely atop a clump of grass. They were shoeless caddies with magic toes at work for their golfers.

These amenities, that were already in place, would serve as the framework of the tourism industry until the foreign investment community could explore the expansion opportunities for building hotels and developing beaches along the beautiful coastline of the South China Sea. A few miles north of Saigon was the coastal city of Vung Tau. It was a popular spot among the Vietnamese. Further to the north, in the Central Highlands, was the city of Dalat, known for its cool temperatures and beautiful, mountainous terrain.

During "peace time" there were several opportunities to visit various parts of the country. Those trips were always via helicopters flown by South Vietnamese pilots. Although there was a cease fire in place, there was always that lingering feeling in the back of my mind that there may be someone down in the jungle, who did not get the memo.

Now that the "endless" war was over, South Vietnam began preparing plans to attract and welcome thousands of tourists to their war-ravaged land. How do you launch such a program? Almost 60,00 Americans died, thousands wounded, tens of thousands of Vietnamese perished, unknown numbers were missing in action and there remained POW's in North and South Vietnam. In the US there had been little support for this conflict. The anti-war movement had been in full swing, with huge anti-war demonstrations throughout the US.

Once the war ended the US Congress voted to slash the funding for military and economic aid to Vietnam. After supporting South Vietnam for so many years, the decision by the US to implement these cuts was the start of a ticking time bomb and would soon become another piece in the puzzle that would mark the end for South Vietnam.

In spite of this dramatic shift in support, the South Vietnamese Government began to plan for tourism and foreign investment. We at Pan Am were cautiously optimistic about the rapidly unfolding developments and began planning sales and marketing programs accordingly.

Shortly after the Cease Fire Agreement was implemented, I was contacted by the Special Assistant to President Thieu. The purpose of the meeting was to discuss an arrangement to lease a Pan Am Boeing 707. The aircraft registry was N704PA. This particular plane was removed from service and parked in the Arizona desert. The lease agreement would include Pan Am pilots who would operate the airplane. This is known in the industry as a wet lease. The flight attendants would be Vietnamese. Prior to positioning the airplane in Saigon, the crew ferried the plane to Hong Kong for maintenance service and cabin modification. The forward cabin was reconfigured along the lines of Air Force One. The first order of business was for the president to fly around the world to express his appreciation to all the allies that supported South Vietnam during the war. The final stop was San Clemente, California where he would meet with President Nixon.

During the San Clemente meeting it was reported that Nixon apparently assured President Thieu that the United States would be ready to support and defend South Vietnam again, should the North Vietnamese violate the agreement and resume military action against the South. This post war policy, in my opinion, was doomed from the start. From a practical standpoint, it was not politically possible to again deploy American combat troops to Vietnam. The ink on the signed Cease Fire Agreement was barely dry and already there was talk of possibly sending troops back to Vietnam. That simply was not going to happen.

Chatting with Ambassador Ellsworth Bunker at an American Chamber of Commerce Luncheon meeting at the Majestic Hotel in Saigon. Bunker left Saigon in May 1973. (Author's collection)

Chapter 7
Trouble on the Horizon

Now that the war was "over," drastic cuts in US military aid were implemented. Cuts in economic aid were also part of the overall reduction of support for South Vietnam. These adjustments marked the beginning of a major shift in the postwar planning strategy, not only for South Vietnam but also for the North Vietnamese. It represented an open invitation to the North Vietnamese to dramatically revise their military strategy as well. Prior to the Cease Fire Agreement, the sounds of war were heard in the distance. Without exception, it was a nightly occurrence. I would often wonder who was dropping those bombs. I thought about how many people were being killed or wounded by those explosions off in the distance; or maybe they were just dropped at random with the hope of inflicting harm or damage on enemy troops.

Would those awful sounds finally end? I suppose one could call it being completely naive, but I did expect, from that point on, that the distant sounds of bombs would cease. I was wrong. The sounds continued. I initially assumed they would not last much longer, that all would soon be quiet. After all, the war was over.

Nevertheless there was cautious optimism in the air and the general population in South Vietnam went about their day-to-day business with a new sense of hope. By June of 1973, all US troops had left South Vietnam and American POWs were released and returned home to the United States. In Saigon, however, there was no celebration, such as the usual parade to recognize that the war was finally over. Army troops continued to guard all government buildings in the city. From all outward appearances, it was business as usual.

In a word, the Cease Fire Agreement could be described as, fragile. The Agreement was now in effect for almost two years. There were numerous violations during this period and starting in mid January 1975, the outlook for stability and some semblance of a normal relationship with the North was yet to take hold. The nightly bombings and other military actions continued and the Commission responsible for supervising the Peace Accords were reporting the violations but, that was the extent of their actions. This was all exacerbated by the drastic reduction of US aid to South Vietnam and the end result was that the South Vietnamese troops were being redeployed from the northern provinces to the south to protect the city of Saigon. When this major shift in strategy was detected by the North, it was a green light for them to begin their final march to reunification.

The provinces that were once held and secured by the South Vietnamese Army were now there for the taking. The southbound movement by the North Vietnamese began slowly in February and March of 1975 and provinces were being taken with hardly a shot being fired. The map of Vietnam on the wall in my office did not represent a promising picture. Saigon was beginning to look like the end of a funnel. It was time begin planning for what appeared to be the inevitable.

Chapter 8
Operation Babylift

For more than a decade the presence and involvement of American troops and other allied forces created more than just military casualties. One of the most visible and painful consequences of the war was the orphan population. The total number of orphans in South Vietnam may never be known, but it is safe to say it was in the tens of thousands. The process of preparing and transporting orphans for adoption in the US was very arduous. The procedure from start to finish could take months. The adoption agencies in South Vietnam were relentless in their effort to complete the process of finding homes and parents in the United States for the orphans.

Pan Am played a major role in the transportation portion of the adoption program. We worked closely with the various adoption agencies. During that time, we were running twice-weekly Boeing 747 service from Saigon to San Francisco, with intermediate stops in Manila, Guam, and Honolulu. There was an ongoing need to recruit volunteers to escort the babies to the US. As a recruiting incentive, we supplied complimentary transportation to the volunteer escorts.

C5-A taking off from Saigon, April 4, 1975, with 243 Vietnamese orphans. Total passengers on board was 311 plus 17 crew. Total fatalities 153.(US Air Force photo)]

During my first week on the job I was greeted with an up-close and personal look at another aspect of the adoption program. A husband-and-wife team, who were Eastern Airlines employees, arrived in Saigon with an incredible number of boxes containing baby toiletries, medications, and supplies. They had everything, from baby aspirins to diapers. Shortly after their arrival, our airport customer service manager called me. He had a sense of urgency in his voice as he asked me to come to the customs area as soon as possible to resolve a problem. The problem was to obtain clearance of more than twenty-five cartons of supplies for an orphanage in Saigon. Jan and I later became very good friends with Dick and Jodie, the two Eastern Airlines employees, who were dedicated to the adoption program. They would fly all the way from Atlanta, Georgia to Saigon, via a number of intermediate stops, spend two hours on the ground in Saigon, then get back onboard our return flight, and fly all the way back to Atlanta. On this particular day, however, instead of just dropping off a couple dozen boxes of baby supplies, they escorted four orphans back to the United States. Let me just say that, caring for four babies on a twenty-hour trip, is no picnic. By no means was this the last time for such a journey. They would arrive again, a month or so later, with more supplies and return to the USA with more babies for delivery to their new parents who were anxiously waiting for them. Little did I know then that this was just the tip of the iceberg to what lay ahead in the last days before the fall of Saigon when the Operation Babylift Program would begin.

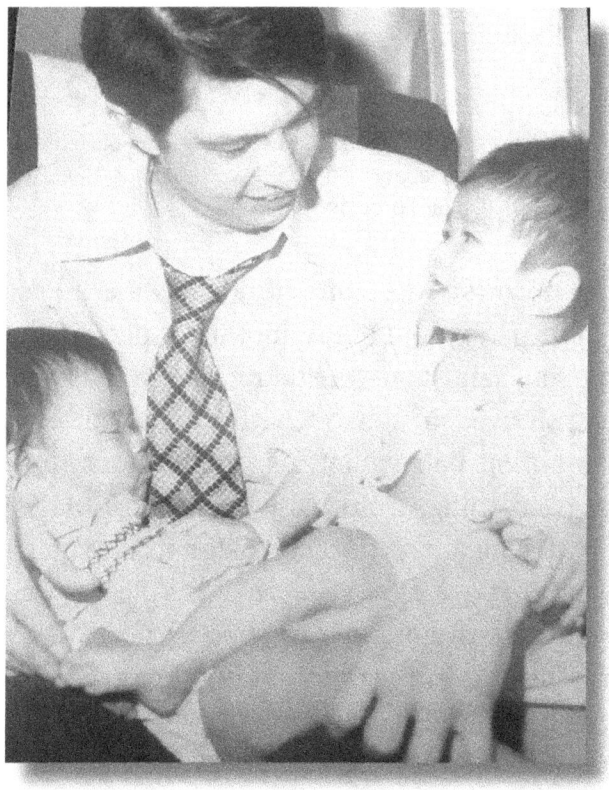

Two arms full - Operation Babylift, April 5, 1975, heading for San Francisco. Austin Lee, former Public Relations Manager, Pan Am Hong Kong (photo Austin Lee collection)

The movement of orphans would soon be taken to an historical, new level. During the painful and protracted years of the Vietnam conflict the presence of not only American troops, but also military personnel from other nations, resulted in a significant number of orphans. The orphanages faced the task of not only caring for the children but also with the tedious task of finishing the process of adoption. The majority of the orphans were adopted by families in the US, but a number of them found homes in other countries as well.

At the time of the C5-A crash on April 4, 1975, South Vietnam was spiraling into complete collapse. One could say that this tragic accident was the beginning of the final days for South Vietnam. The Cease Fire Agreement, that was supposed to end the war and bring peace and stability to Vietnam, turned out to be only a temporary halt to the fighting. Ironically, this was the prediction of the South Vietnam administration. Now that all US combat troops were withdrawn (except for those being held as POW's) and the US Congress had slashed both military and economic aid to Vietnam, it was just a matter of time before the history of the Vietnam War would be written.

The atmosphere throughout the country was now becoming extremely tense. The complete US withdrawal of our combat troops and the drastic reduction of aid to South Vietnam sent a clear signal to North Vietnam that the time had arrived for liberating the South. There was no question about it, the situation was unraveling quickly.

My US Embassy contacts kept me up to date with what was happening. I also kept informed by tuning into the BBC on my shortwave radio. I would stick pins in the map I had on the office wall. The picture that was developing was clear and indicated that it was simply a matter of time. When I connected the dots, I could see that Saigon was looking like the end of a funnel. Provinces and cities in the north central portions of South Vietnam were falling like dominoes. Refugees were fleeing as the communist troops continued their march south without firing a shot.

The tragedy of the C5-A crash made headlines around the world. Young, innocent children were sucked out of the rear cargo door of the giant plane. Their lives were over in just a matter of seconds.

Prior to the ill-fated departure of the C-5A, the US Air Force used some of our ground equipment to service and load the huge planes. As I watched the loading of over two-hundred children onto the huge airplane, in the back of my mind I began to feel uneasy about their safety. There was just something about that entire scene that caused me to feel sad and concerned. Once the aircraft was buttoned up and began rolling down the runway, I watched as it took off and headed east until it was almost out of sight.

After returning to my airport office, about fifteen minutes later, I heard an unusual amount of helicopter traffic overhead. I returned to the tarmac and there it was, about a mile or so away, columns of black smoke. I said to myself, "No it can't be the C5-A. Please don't let it be the C-5A." But as it turned out, it was the C-5A. It was such a sad and tragic scene. Just a few minutes earlier I had watched as the children and their medical volunteers boarded that flight. Obviously, it was too soon to know the number of fatalities and survivors. Regardless of the number of fatalities, it would be too many. I immediately called the American Embassy and informed Eva Kim, the Ambassador's Secretary, about what had just happened.

It was a gruesome scene at the site of the wreckage of the C5-A . The aircraft crashed about a mile short of the runway as the crew tried to return to Saigon after the aft cargo door malfunctioned, blew off, severing some of the hydraulic lines, and resulting in serious control problems. The pilot, Captain Dennis "Bud" Traynor, and copilot Captain Tilford Harp, struggled to regain control in order to return to Tan Son Nhut. They were able to maintain a controlled descent and begin the approach to runway 25L at Tan Son Nhut; but despite all of their heroic efforts, the giant C5-A touched down short of the runway in a rice paddy and broke into four pieces. The fuel caught fire, along with some of the wreckage.

Loading babies, Operation Babylift, April 5, 1975. Some were survivors of the C5-A crash. That's me, upper left, adjusting my sunglasses. (Author's collection)

The crash of the C5-A was, for me, another unforgettable moment. Rescue workers in helicopters frantically shuttled survivors from the crash site to the hospital.

The flight had a total of 311 passengers and 17 crew members. There were 153 fatalities and 175 survivors. Almost fifty percent of the passengers lost their lives. When the news of the C5-A hit the worldwide media, it really hit home to Robert Macauley. This tragic incident became the catalyst for the formation of the AmeriCares Charity. Within twenty-four hours after the crash, I received word from Operations Control at Kennedy Airport that two Pan Am 747's were heading to Saigon. Their mission was to rescue hundreds of orphans, including the survivors of the deadly C5-A crash. I later learned that Macauley was so moved by the tragic event that he mortgaged his New Canaan, Connecticut home to finance one of the 747 charters. The survivors of the crash included the children and volunteers from a number of orphanages in South Vietnam including, Friends for All Children (FFAC) and the Holt International Adoption Agency.

Bill Cowden, Regional Managing Director Southeast Asia, at plane side during the boarding of some 300 babies onto the 747 at Tan Son Nhut, 24 hours after C5-A crash. Destination, San Francisco. April 5, 1975 (Author's collection)

In 1981, Pope John Paul II asked Macauley to help deliver medical supplies to Poland, which was then under martial law. Macauley was successful in obtaining $1.5 million in medical supplies from more than a dozen countries and arranged for the airlift to Poland in March 1982. In 1990 Macauley told The Toronto Star, "Someone will always give nine reasons why it can't be done; just mow 'em down. Make things happen."

John McGhee was the Director of Marketing for the Far East based in Tokyo. Following is his recollection of the role that he and other Pan Am staffers played in Operation Babylift. (Source - Pan Am Aviation History Through the Words of Its People - by James Baldwin & Jeff Kriendler)

It was April 1975. We were pulling our troops out of Vietnam. I was in my 12th year with Pan American World Airways and I lived in Tokyo, Japan.

In Tokyo, we lived in a Pan Am compound with fellow employees and carpooled to work. As was the tradition in many overseas posts, we worked a half day on Saturday. Because of the International Date Line, we needed Saturday to see what went on at the Pan Am Building Headquarters in New York the day before and if necessary, respond to them when they opened for business on Monday morning.

One Saturday, Malcolm MacDonald, Regional Managing Director; James P. O'Hagan, Director of Maintenance; and I, Director of Marketing, all arrived at the Pan Am office. We learned that the Guam flight, a Boeing 747 had been canceled and was going to be worked as charter flight to Tan Son Nhut Airport in Saigon to pick up orphaned babies (American fathers, Vietnamese mothers). It was going to be a voluntary mission running in a war zone, so the company could not assign a cabin crew; they all would have to volunteer, and several did. Jim and I said we would go as did two sales staff from

Honolulu who happened to be in Japan for orientation and training. I asked our Japanese reservations staff if anyone wanted to volunteer and five of them agreed to help as well. Keep in mind the Vietnam conflict was not Japan's war and the sympathy that one might have as a US citizen was not in evidence locally.

We drove to Haneda Airport. Once there, we had the insight to take a supply of boxes normally held in the check-in area to accommodate passengers who arrived with too many bits and pieces. We left on our seven-hour flight to Saigon shortly thereafter. While en route, we placed the check-in boxes on the floor between the seat back and seat and put a pillow and a blanket in each box. This was where we were going to place the babies on the return flight.

As we flew, we talked about a US Air Force C-5A Galaxy that crashed the day before with babies on board. We also had read an article in the US military newspaper, Stars & Stripes, where World Airways President Ed Daly was aboard a Boeing 727 in Danang that had started its takeoff roll under heavy fire with the back airstairs still down. A picture was snapped of Daly using a 45-caliber pistol to fend off other people trying to board the plane. This led to concern that our planes would be rushed by people trying to leave Saigon before the North captured the city. As a safety measure, Jim O'Hagan climbed down from the first-class compartment to lock the belly doors from inside Once on the ground, Jim and I had no weapons so we positioned ourselves with fire extinguishers at L-1 thinking we could deny entrance by spraying them.

Anxiously we waited; the door opened and we were pleased to see an orderly assembly of people including Bill Cowden the Regional Managing Director and Al Topping, Director of Vietnam. Buses drove to the aircraft and we all ran down the stairs. A baby or two with his or her ditty bag of possessions were put into our arms and we ran up the stairs and placed a baby in a box. After what seemed little more than an hour, we had 350 souls onboard, but none were visible. Against policy, we also took the Vietnamese wife and two children of the Saigon Maintenance Manager onboard. The Vietnamese had confiscated their US passports, but it seemed like the right thing to do.

Once airborne we began to feed the babies starting at the front of the cabin and working our way back. By the time we had them all fed, diarrhea had broken out either from the boarding excitement or the unfamiliar formula, so our next job was to change 350 diapers starting from front to back. After several hours of this the only place to get a breath of good air was in the toilets. We touched down a 3:00 a.m. at Yokota, a US Air Force Base near Tokyo. Japanese Public health Inspectors came aboard and found that measles was on board and requested that all personnel deplaning in Japan go into a two-week quarantine period. Fortunately, my title and the prestige of Pan Am supplied enough pressure to convince the Public Health officials to appoint me responsible for letting them know of any illness. Wrapping the maintenance manager's wife and children in blankets, we slipped them off the plane and into a Pan Am station wagon that had come up from Haneda Airport to meet the flight. We knew we were bringing them into the country illegally, but after all this was war.

A crew of Air Force nurses took over the responsibility of caring for the babies as the flight left with a fresh Pan Am operating crew. On April 5, 1975 President Ford met the flight, which was designated Clipper 1742, in

San Francisco and welcomed these young souls into the United States.

Once back at the Pan Am compound, we reported to the Managing Director that we had sneaked the family of the Saigon employee into the country but felt that no one had seen us. He advised us to report it to the Japanese Immigration authorities the next day which we did. The next day Stars & Stripes had a photo on the front page with the headline "Mystery Woman Enters Japan." It seemed we had caused an international incident and as a consequence, had to formally apologize with cap in hand to the Japanese Government. A simple enough punishment for what we still think was the right thing to do.

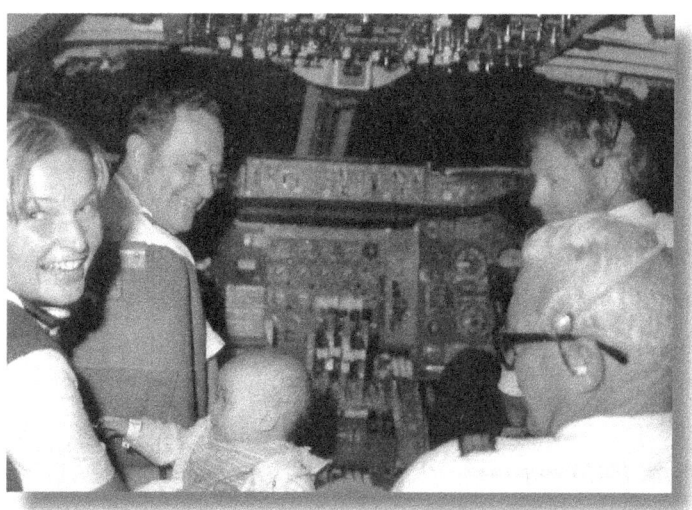

Flight Attendant Paula Helfrich in the cockpit with one of the little ones during Operation Babylift.

Over the years I often wondered if we did the proper thing by removing the babies from the country of their birth, but the prevailing thought at the time was that they would be killed or severely ostracized as *social misfits, being children of American fathers and Vietnamese mothers.*

I felt fully exonerated when in April 2005 I attended the 30th reunion of The Last Flight Out held in Washington, DC. Former Pan Am staff mingled with the babies, now young adults. Several were medical doctors, one was a CNN broadcaster, and there were other bright and accomplished young Americans who just happened to have been born in Vietnam."

Chapter 9
The End Is Near

It was the second week in April of 1975 and the situation in South Vietnam was rapidly deteriorating. There was a feeling of uncertainty from one day to the next. The C5-A crash was the tipping point. The level of desperation to escape was building by the hour. Tens of thousands of South Vietnamese civilians were looking for a way out. Time was running out and I was at a loss as to how we were going to evacuate our staff and their "immediate families."

The company made a commitment to evacuate each Pan Am employee and members of their immediate family. I sensed that our employees were beginning to lose faith in me, because I was unable to share with them my plan for their evacuation. The options on how to escape the inevitable collapse of South Vietnam were rapidly vanishing.

In spite of all the chaos and uncertainty, the South Vietnamese Government, now a mere remnant, was still in control; therefore, the immigration policy was still in effect. The policy would require several weeks to process the required documentation to leave the country. There was simply no time to do that. So now what?

As for Jan and me, this would not be a problem because, as American citizens, we could leave at any time. I had decided in early March of 1975 that, since the days ahead looked bleak and fraught with danger, to send Jan home to San Francisco. Once she left Vietnam, I was then able to devote my full attention to the many challenges and uncertainties in the critical days ahead.

My number one priority was to figure out how to legally come up with an evacuation plan for our employees and their immediate families, so that they could leave the country before it was too late; a process that normally could take up to two or three months. Secondly, it was absolutely essential that I convey a sincere sense of hope and trust to our staff that they would be evacuated before the collapse of their homeland. One can only imagine how emotionally difficult it must have been for them to continue working under those stressful circumstances.

The pressure and stress were building by the day and by the hour; it came from everywhere. Our sales office was packed every day. The phones and telex machines were going non-stop. Ambassador Martin was suggesting that we increase the frequency of our flights from twice weekly to three flights per week. That was simply not going to happen. It would be difficult to justify the increase in operations because the existing twice weekly scheduled operation was, at best, averaging a load factor of only about fifty percent. The impact on our loads was directly related to the problems the Vietnamese citizens had in legally processing the paperwork in order to leave the country.

In terms of actual reservations made, our advance bookings were running at 100% and higher. The inflated booking issue was caused by local Vietnamese citizens who made reservations on every flight in anticipation that friends or relatives in the US who would arrange for prepaid tickets. The tickets, for their travel to the United States, would be wired to Saigon. This was such a sad and gut-wrenching situation. For the most part,

The last United States Ambassador in South Vietnam, Ambassador Graham Martin.

the prepaid tickets never came, but the reservation requests continued unabated.

There was one scene that occurred at the airport that I will never forget. An American civilian had returned to Saigon in an effort to arrange for his girlfriend to return with him to the United States. Apparently, he was unsuccessful in getting the required documentation to allow her departure. Nevertheless, she was at the airport at our departure gate to say goodbye. Suddenly, instead of the typical hug and farewell kiss, she lunged at him and clawed him across the face with her fingernails. Blood flowed from his entire face. The scene was not only graphic, to say the least, but it was so sad. She was crying and screaming and became hysterical. We were eventually able to separate them and quickly got him onboard. Once onboard, the flight attendants were able to supply adequate first aid and stopped the bleeding prior to departure.

Now it was time to begin preparing for the arrival of two special Babylift Pan Am 747 charters. There was much to do. These two airplanes would be the way out for almost seven-hundred children, many of them survivors of the C5-A crash.

During the previous two plus years, Pan Am was an active participant in the movement of orphans from South Vietnam to primarily the United States. We worked with a number of orphanages and nurseries in Saigon, such as the Holt Adoption Agency and Friends For All Children (FFAC). Under normal circumstances, children would travel in small groups, usually not to exceed eight or ten per flight. Suddenly, with the crash of the C5-A and Saigon in the crosshairs of advancing communist troops, any sense of normalcy had vanished. Representing the FFAC Nursery was one of the most dedicated individuals I have ever met, Rosemary Taylor. She was relentless in her mission of caring for the children. Within twenty-four hours of the tragic C5-A accident, we operated the two 747 charters. Rosemary and her volunteers prepared over three-hundred children for evacuation. It was remarkable. Rosemary was lovingly known as the mother of a thousand children.

My first recommendation to Operations Control in New York was that, under no circumstances should we have both airplanes on the ground in Saigon at the same time. Why? The reason was due to the fact that two 747 airplanes, parked on the tarmac, would create a highly visible target and would be at risk of being destroyed, or suffering serious indiscriminate damage by rocket fire. The terrain in the area around Saigon was very flat and the four-story height of the tail of a 747 would be visible from a long distance away. I was also concerned and absolutely certain that practically everything we were preparing and planning to do was probably known by friend and foe alike. Then there was the real possibility of a security perimeter breakdown and hundreds of people overrunning our planes. During this time hundreds of souls were camped around the airport perimeter.

That being said on April 5, 1975, we worked the two 747 charters. It was another one of those days I'll never forget. The folks at the orphanages were probably up all night preparing the children for the flights to the United States the next morning. Pan Am operations was in high gear setting up the special charters. We needed volunteer cockpit crews and flight attendants. Additionally, since a number of the children and babies had health issues, it was necessary to have volunteer doctors and nurses onboard to care for them during the long flight across the Pacific to the West Coast of the United States.

I barely slept the night before the charter flights; but I prayed a lot. My mind was going through a myriad of troubling thoughts. What if, during the night, the flights had to be cancelled because of sudden increase in the level of hostilities? What if we could not get enough volunteer crew members to work the flights? What if the South Vietnamese Government had decided on a change of policy and announced that the waivers for the adoption program were cancelled? Finally I decided to toss those negative thoughts out of my mind and focus only on the positive things and place the rest of it in God's hands.

It was a serious and scary time and those flights simply had to operate as planned. Too many precious lives were at stake. Finally the two 747's were in position. One in Manila and the second one would be coming from Tokyo via Hong Kong for the operation out of Saigon on April 5, 1975.

At this point in time no one knew the cause of the C5-A crash. Was it rocket fire from the ground or was it sabotage? Was it simply a mechanical malfunction? On that memorable day as I watched the first 747 on final approach to Tan Son Nhut Airport, my heart was thumping like a drum. What a beautiful sight! I watched as the first plane touched down. I watched with silent joy and some fear. Fear, because this was just the first of two parts. Joy, because, if we could successfully complete this operation without incident, we could save many lives. My thoughts were, "So far so good. Thank you, Lord." As soon as the airplane stopped, at a special remote parking area, we began loading the babies. As a precautionary measure, believe or not, we performed random baby body searches—just to make sure there were no explosives hidden under their diapers. Nothing was left to chance. As I searched and carried some of the babies up the stairs and on to the airplane, I wanted to tell them what we were doing. Of course they had no idea what was going on, but I hoped someday they would know the entire story and understand what took place during those final days in South Vietnam.

On board the airplane, on the seats, were row after row of bassinets and cardboard file cartons, serving as bassinets; each had a seatbelt over the top. There were bassinets on the floor between seats as well; another scene etched in my brain forever. Many of the children were in bandages and casts as a result of the injuries suffered in the C5-A accident. Prior to departure I took one last walk through the cabin. The crying and screaming was ear-piercing. It was as if over three-hundred children were inoculated simultaneously. There was also the stench of soiled diapers flowing through the air in the cabin. There are times in life when one gets goose bumps. That was one of those moments for me.

As the first 747 with over three hundred onboard rolled down the runway for takeoff, the second plane was on final approach for landing—another beautiful sight. Another load of over three hundred would be boarding, and we were geared up and ready to do it all over again. Padding the infants down for possible explosives, bassinets, cardboard file boxes, seat belts over the top and, yes, the screaming along with the stench of soiled diapers.

As we dispatched the second flight, I watched it ascend into the clear blue sky and head east. I had just one thought; I wished that we could have included our staff and their families on that flight.

This was a memorable event for many obvious reasons. I will always remember the support and involvement from my boss, Bill Cowden. Bill was the Regional Managing Director for the Southeast Asia Region and was based in Hong Kong. He flew into Saigon from Hong Kong and was with us for a part of the Babylift operation. It didn't matter to him that he was under the weather and not feeling well; he was there, and I'll always remember his unwavering support and concern for those caught in this desperate situation. He was a great guy, terrific boss, a good friend, and his support was invaluable to me.

I knew that time was running out and my plan to evacuate our employees was far from complete. There were many moving parts and so little time. During those final weeks we did some things that were not exactly according to our departure procedures. For example, one of our airport customer service staff, whose job it was to make the final check at the door with the flight attendant, simply handed over the passenger manifest, stepped inside, closed the door and off she went to Guam to be processed as a refugee.

Meanwhile, in Danang, South Vietnam's second largest city, chaos was in a full free-fall. Ed Daly, the president of World Airways landed in a B-727 to evacuate as many women and children as possible. In the end, only a handful of women and children made it onboard. As the plane came to a stop on the tarmac, the situation suddenly turned ugly. South Vietnamese troops began storming the plane through the aft staircase. The troops just kept coming. Daly was at the top of the stairs armed with a revolver and a cane trying to stop the stampede, but to no avail. The plane began to taxi toward the runway, cutting across taxiways and a chain link fence. All the while a crowd, consisting of mostly men and South Vietnamese troops in civilian clothes, was chasing the aircraft down the runway. Some were on motor bikes. Somehow, in the midst of all the chaos and stampede of desperation, it was also reported that a couple of guys managed to climb up into the landing gear compartment. Another person was clinging to the rear stairs as the airplane took off with the stairs still extended. Unfortunately, he could not hold on for long, and fell to his death into the South China Sea. I was at the airport when that flight landed in Saigon. The scene I witnessed will be forever imprinted in my mind. As the jet came to a stop, blood was flowing from the wheel well where the bodies were crushed as the landing gear retracted after takeoff from Danang.

One can only imagine what it was like onboard that flight from Danang to Saigon. A Boeing 727, with an all-economy seating configuration, would normally have a capacity of about one-hundred ten seats. On this particular trip there were more than two hundred in the cabin. It was also reported that more than one-hundred souls were in the baggage compartment in the belly of the airplane. In all probability that World Airways 727 should never have gotten off the ground; but in their desperate effort to leave Danang the crew taxied rapidly to the runway and went right through a chain link fence. They damaged the leading edge flaps, but they continued, and it was wheels up heading south to Saigon. Without question this Boeing 727 aircraft, with more than three-hundred onboard, would go down in history as carrying the largest passenger load ever—not to mention the desperate souls who were in the landing gear compartment who perished, and the one who could no longer cling to the extended aft stair, falling to his death into the South China Sea. Upon arrival in Saigon, the

South Vietnamese troops who were on board disembarked, left the airport, blending in with the Saigon population.

It was a sad day for so many. Fear of the advancing enemy troops had now gripped the city and people were desperately seeking ways to escape before it was too late. A number of general managers from other multinational corporations were booking reservations on our flights for their employees. In spite of the fact that Saigon was falling, the remnant of what remained of the government was still in control of the exit visa process. Normally it would take weeks to process the paperwork, but unfortunately, we were running out of time.

In April of 1975 we had sixty-two Vietnamese employees. Jerry Fedorak and I were the only two Americans on staff. Jerry was our Maintenance Manager. It was now the middle of April and I knew that time was getting short. The fuse had been lit and I paced the floor every night trying to figure out a way to evacuate our employees and their immediate families. Our Headquarters in New York and Pacific Division Headquarters in Honolulu gave me the approval to develop a plan for getting our staff and their immediate families out. The problem was I still did not know how I was going to pull it off. I could feel the fear and anxiety in the air emanating from our staff. At this point I knew they were probably losing hope and trust in me. I could only tell them to have faith and trust me, but I could not tell them how or when we would be closing down the operation. I could not tell them because frankly, at that point, I did not know. In the back of my mind I had one thought; that somehow, with or without documentation, I was going to get them to the airport, onto the plane and out of the country.

Panic in Saigon was escalating. The United States Air Force was using C-141 jet transports around the clock unloading tons of various supplies for, what I would describe, the remnants of the South Vietnamese Army. During the peak of the war, the South Vietnamese Army was supposedly one million strong. In

April 1975 that number was dramatically reduced to probably only a few thousand. The United States was continuing to provide them with weapons and related supplies in spite of the level of hostilities and chaos. Sadly, the reality was that all of the aid would end up in the hands of the communist troops poised for their final push into Saigon.

As the military supplies were unloaded onto the tarmac, the planes were used to evacuate the Vietnamese and their families who once worked for the United States Government and US Government contractors.

Our downtown sales office was packed every day. It seemed as though everyone in Saigon was trying to make a reservation on Pan Am. A significant number of Vietnamese women were waiting and hoping that the father of their child or children would send them a prepaid ticket for travel from Saigon to the United States. So in anticipation of their ticket coming through by wire, they would secure a booking on our flight. As a result, during those tumultuous final weeks, our flights were heavily booked on paper but in reality, they were leaving with a fifty or sixty percent no-show factor.

Yes, indeed it was now crunch time. I had great concerns about what the American Embassy was planning as an evacuation operation. In early April I moved out of our house downtown and shared a trailer with a USAF Officer at Tan Son Nhut Airport. This relocation was critical since it provided options that I would not have if I continued living in the city. Some of the options included immediate access to an aircraft, and direct communications with the United States and Vietnamese military personnel assigned to the airport.

The American Embassy, under the leadership of Ambassador Graham Martin and his staff, was developing an evacuation plan for the Americans as well as the Vietnamese who were working for the United States Government at various facilities throughout South Vietnam. I attended a couple of the planning meetings hosted by embassy staffers. As we discussed the details of the plan, my first thought was that it was much too risky, and I did not see how the plan would work for our employees and their families. The plan called for designating a number of rooftops throughout the city where evacuees would assemble, wait for pick up by helicopters, and then flown to the US Navy ships waiting offshore in the South China Sea. I was concerned about this plan.

So time was running out and I still did not know how to get our people out on time. I did not know how much time we had. I was getting little sleep, and everyone was wondering when I was going to let them know our evacuation plan. I was also hearing from former employees. They had been laid off two years ago and were asking me to help them get out before it was too late. Not only were former Pan Am employees looking for help and a way out, but also several were calling and seeking help in evacuating their people.

In one dramatic evacuation move the Flying Tiger Line, a cargo operator, sent some of their people out in cargo containers from Saigon to Tokyo or perhaps it was Hong Kong, or maybe both. Flying Tigers had all they could handle and then some. All of the American expatriates and others were desperately trying to salvage their personal effects. They had bought lots of Asian goodies over the years; those possessions were important to them and they wanted to ship as many of them as possible to the United States. Fortunately, Jan and I had shipped about ninety percent of our personal and household effects out earlier.

As the panic mode began to intensify, I could sense that our employees were starting to believe that I did not have a plan and probably was not going to get them out on time. This was understandable because I still did not know how it was going to happen. I continued to tell them to have faith and to trust me.

Chapter 10
Final Departure

In spite of all the chaos and uncertainty, we continued to operate our two weekly flights on Tuesdays and Thursdays. Due to what appeared to be pent up demand, Ambassador Martin again asked me if we could increase our frequency of service into Saigon. Regretfully, it was difficult to justify because our two scheduled flights were leaving with a load factor of under fifty percent. So we maintained our normal schedule of operation.

As I continued to have sleepless nights, pacing the trailer floor, I could not get the map on my office wall out of my mind. The picture I continued to see was that Saigon was at the end of a funnel. It was not a pretty picture. What I saw was the North Vietnamese troops pouring through that funnel directly into downtown Saigon.

Then suddenly it hit me. It became clear to me that Saigon would fall on May 1, 1975. Why May first? That is May Day, a major communist holiday; and what day would be better than May Day to triumphantly march into downtown Saigon and raise the North Vietnamese flag on the roof of the Presidential Palace? I began racking my brain, trying to figure out a way to get our people out. I was feeling pressure from all sides. Pan Am headquarters was pressing for a plan. They wanted to know when we should cease operations. The FAA was planning to order all US carriers to terminate all commercial flights into South Vietnam because the level of hostilities had reached a dangerous level.

It was April 8, 1975, about 9:00 a.m., and I was in our downtown office when I heard a horrendous roar of an airplane. It sounded as if the roof of the building had been ripped off. Then, a few seconds later, I heard an explosion. The office was crowded with customers and everyone was screaming, and my secretary came running into my office yelling, "Mr. Topping, the Viet Cong are here!" At that moment I thought it was all over and that I had waited too long. I thought, "Oh no, not now!" We had a scheduled flight that day, coming in from Manila.

Within minutes after the incident Saigon erupted into chaos. I dashed out of the office and headed for the airport. The streets were gridlocked with motor bikes, cyclos and cars and it seemed like it took forever to get to the airport. Panic was definitely in the air. By the time I got to the airport, I found out that Saigon was not under attack. The news about the incident came to me via my embassy handheld radio. A South Vietnamese Air Force pilot, who was supposed to be on a routine bombing run to attack North Vietnamese troops, instead decided to bomb the Presidential Palace in Saigon. We later learned that First Lieutenant Nguyen Thanh Trung was the pilot and had been a Viet Cong agent since 1969. He was hailed as a hero by the North Vietnamese.

The word on the wire services, however, was that Saigon appeared to be under attack. This news immediately went global, so I knew that Jan, our families back in the States, and those at the Pan Am headquarters would be extremely concerned. They would also be concerned about the safety and wellbeing of our staff. In those days, there was no internet nor texting capabilities, but there was the good old, reliable Pan Am telex system and co-workers who could relay messages to Jan and my Mom. In San Francisco my former secretary, Patsy Yamamoto, would relay messages to Jan. In New York, my good friend, Jeff Kriendler, VP of Corporate Communications, would be in touch with my Mom to assure her that, in spite of what was being reported by local TV networks, I was okay and would soon be home. At the same time those messages were relayed at ground zero in Saigon, I was praying a lot. I was hoping that somehow, we were going to make the evacuation happen and that we would get our staff out before it was too late.

After the attack on the Presidential Palace, my immediate concern was whether we would be able to operate our regularly scheduled flight. Due to the attack on the palace, Pan Am Headquarters informed me that our flight was placed on hold in Manila and that it may, in fact, be cancelled. Frankly, this was a moment that was totally unexpected. Our flight was scheduled to leave Manila for Saigon. Then the dreaded message came over the telex machine from Pan Am Operations in New York stating that, due to the current level of hostilities in South Vietnam, they were planning to cancel the flight.

When I received news of that possibility, I was on the phone immediately with New York, Hong Kong, Honolulu, and Manila begging and pleading with them not to cancel the flight. I told them that cancelling the flight was unacceptable; that it must operate. It was a critical time for moving people out of Saigon. On that particular day we had three-hundred people at the airport waiting to board the flight back to the US. Based on the current situation in South Vietnam, those passengers would not have a problem with a delayed departure; there would be no complaints, whatsoever. We just had to do whatever was necessary to operate the flight. I was not about to allow a cancellation of the operation. We would have a riot on our hands. The airport terminal was packed. Saigon was, for all practical purposes, surrounded by enemy troops, and our passengers, along with tens of thousands of others, were desperate to get out of the country. The flight must operate.

After many conference calls followed by much debate, the flight was reinstated and five hours behind schedule. Finally, we were buttoned up with everyone onboard and ready for departure. There were no complaints about the delay. Those passengers were glad to be heading back to the United States. Most of the passengers were Americans, some Vietnamese and yes, still more orphans destined to various cities in the United States for adoption. As I watched that magnificent 747 lift off and turn to the East, I felt sad that our employees were not onboard. Why? Time was running out.

Then a major turn of events happened. We received word that, due to the level of hostilities in the country, the FAA was advising all US carriers that they must terminate all commercial flights in and out of Saigon. That meant Pan Am would not be allowed to operate any more flights. Things were now beginning to unravel. There were only a few days left to pull off the evacuation. Our employees were still unaware of when or how I would get them out.

On April 22, 1975, I thought the most significant piece of the puzzle had finally fallen into place. Our final departure was now officially approved. We would operate flight 842 on April 24th as a U.S. government charter from Manila to Saigon and back to Manila. So from a flight operations standpoint we were set. This approval for the final departure was the result of Herculean efforts by Pan Am senior management and the FAA in Washington, D.C. These negotiations reached the level of the Oval Office in the White House. When that special waiver was granted, all of us in Saigon knew at that moment that the end was eminent. But I still did not know how I could legally get our employees out of the country. Incidentally, during those final days of planning the evacuation, my telex communications with my boss and others were in code. I was using the company code book to maintain confidentially about our evacuation plans.

When our Human Resources supervisor presented me with a list of our employees and their immediate families, there were almost seven-hundred names on the list. "These are the names of our employees and their 'immediate' family members,'" he said. This is where the cultural differences dramatically came into play. The interpretation of immediate family in the Asian culture is completely different from the western culture. In Asia, the immediate family is, simply put, everybody in the family is the immediate family—end of story.

This was not the time for me to be the bearer of bad news. No, not now; people were desperate and afraid. They still did not know if Pan Am was going to get them out in time. They were fearful of what could happen if they were unable to escape. I could sense that they were not sure about the Pan Am plan to get them out before it was too late. So I immediately set up a staff meeting with our managers to discuss the "immediate family" issue. I explained to them that it would not be possible for me to select which family members would evacuate and which would have to stay behind. I also knew that those who stayed behind would face the real possibility of torturous treatment, or even death, in "re-education camps."

It was most likely at that time when I decided to try something that would probably require divine intervention. What if I could convince the government of South Vietnam to grant me permission, on behalf of Pan Am, to adopt our employees and their immediate family members? I'm certain that, at that point in time, had I shared this idea with the staff, they probably would have believed I had "lost it." They would probably have thought that the stress had finally taken its toll and their Pan Am director didn't have a clue about how to save them from the communist invasion.

So that night, as I was pacing the floor in the trailer and praying for protection and wisdom, I realized and decided that this would probably be our only hope. Why not give it a shot? Under normal circumstances it would take several months to process all the paperwork and related procedures in order to get final approval for an orphan to travel to the United States for adoption. Now, orphans by the hundreds were being approved to leave the country at once and normal procedures and regulations were waived. Our staff were not orphans, but they must leave the country before it was too late. My only thought was, "I've got to get them out." That was when I decided to do whatever was necessary to get approval to adopt our employees and their immediate family members.

I asked our Human Resources supervisor to go to the office of the Foreign Ministry and find out how we could take advantage of the waivers for the adoption program. He was instructed to secure all necessary documentation that would legally authorize me and the company to take full responsibility for the wellbeing of our staff and the members of their immediate families. He returned a couple of hours later with a large pile of documents to be filled out. Once the documents were completed and I had signed them all, he returned the following day with the seal of approval from the Ministry. By the way, since all the paperwork was in the Vietnamese language, I was clueless as to what I had signed up for. I just started signing and kept on signing until the entire package of documents was signed and stamped. Time was short and getting shorter by the hour.

I continued to be concerned about the evacuation options planned by the American Embassy, so that is why I decided it was necessary to find an alternate evacuation plan. First of all how do I decide and work out the logistics of sending some three hundred of our staff and family members to rooftop helicopter pads throughout the city? How will I keep track of this movement? What happens if some choppers stop flying and people are stranded on a rooftop? How would I know who made it to the offshore ships, or who didn't make it, and when, where, and how would we meet up again?

Rumors were rampant during those final days. Fortunately for me, I had some reliable sources on the ground, and I was able to keep up with the latest progress of enemy troop movements via the BBC on my shortwave radio. Tension continued to rapidly heat up.

For several weeks I was communicating with Regional and Division Headquarters via coded messages, so our staff did not know that I had already made the decision to operate our final departure on April 24, 1975. The significance of the date was that it was a day we operated our usual scheduled service from Saigon to the United States. If we planned a special flight on a non-scheduled day, it would become obvious to everyone that Pan Am was ending its Saigon operation. It would send a signal that now for sure it was all over, causing a level of panic and chaos that could have been catastrophic. After seeing what had happened in Danang with the World Airways 727 debacle, I could only imagine what would have happened when many hundreds of people, desperate to flee to safety, stormed a 747.

Our downtown sales office was packed every day with people trying to make a reservation. A number of them continued to hope that the father of their child would wire a prepaid ticket, so that they could actually make a booking on one of our flights. Sadly, in a number of these cases, that prepaid ticket never materialized.

Final details for our evacuation flight were now in place. This special exemption would apply only to the Manila to Saigon and back to Manila sectors. So PA#842 was re-designated as Air Mission #1965/3.

My focus continued to be divided between keeping corporate apprised of the local deteriorating situation and the safe evacuation plan for our Saigon employees.

There were several people and corporate departments concerned about our wellbeing, and their efforts will never be forgotten. They were my boss, Bill Cowden, Regional Managing Director in Hong Kong; Ed Swofford, Vice President, Pacific Division, based in Honolulu; CEO William Seawell, Pan Am Building New York City; Jeff Kriendler, Vice President Corporate Communications, Pan Am Building, New York City; Ken Sitton, Director of Guam; Cal Yuen, Regional Director Security, based in Hong Kong; Jerry Fedorak, Maintenance Manager, Saigon; Jim O'Hagen, Director Line Maintenance, Pacific Division, based in Tokyo; Willard Knapp, Director Human Resources, Pacific Division, based in Honolulu; Operations Control Department, Hangar 14 at JFK; all the pilots and flight attendants who volunteered to operate the Operation Babylift flights during the month of April 1975; and, of course, those who volunteered to work our final departure on April 24th under the command of Captain Bob Berg. The flight attendants on our final departure from Saigon were Pam Taylor, Purser; Valarie Chaulk, Jean Stewart Kelly, Laura Lee Gillespie, Susan Matson, Gudrun Meisner, Tra Duong Iwafuchi, Sissel Donnelly, and Sally Pearl. I just can't say enough about our pilots and flight attendants who volunteered to operate a civilian airliner in an active war zone, risking their own safety. We will be forever grateful.

The situation was developing into an intense dilemma for us. Our reservations operation was turning into a nightmare. Bookings were now approaching one thousand per flight. I knew that those numbers were inflated, but what we did not know was the actual number of passengers, with legitimate reservations, who would actually show up for the flight. In the meantime, I still did not know how many of our employees and their "immediate" family members we were going to have. I needed more time, but time was running out. I was still receiving phone calls and visits from former employees I had laid off two years before. Calls from my counterparts at other corporations continued to come in, asking for help to get their employees out. A number of the expatriates had already left Vietnam and were monitoring the situation in safe havens, such as Hong Kong and Bangkok. There were some who simply left their Vietnamese employees to fend for themselves.

As the chaos and uncertainties continued to escalate, what happened next was not what I needed to deal with. I was feeling as though the walls were closing in, with no windows or doors. How do I reduce the seven-hundred staff and their families to a manageable and realistic number? How do I convey this gut-wrenching message to a fellow employee that some members of his or her family cannot come with us? We were now dealing with life-or-death type of issues. I informed the managers that we have now reached the point where they must make one of the most difficult decisions of their lives; they would have to tell some family members that they would not be able leave with us on our final departure. It was, without a doubt, the most difficult situation I had to deal with during those final hours.

The final hours were now upon us. Saigon was on the brink of turning into a city of bedlam and desperation. The airport was now the main focus of escape. As I was moving about the city the crush of motor bikes and people walking and running was making it almost impossible to drive. When the car stopped at a traffic light people were leaning against the car, peering in at me, giving me looks as if to say, "I guess you're bailing out on us, aren't you?" Those were frightening moments. My greatest fear was that Americans may suddenly become the enemy because, after so many years of support from the United States, we were now fleeing Vietnam like rats from a sinking ship. Very soon, the South Vietnamese people would be on their own. The handwriting was on the wall. The war would finally be over, and the South Vietnamese people would be at the mercy of the communists from North Vietnam. Leaving the South Vietnamese behind, particularly those who worked for American companies or the United States Government, would be at greater risks of suffering unknown hardship. Abandonment was the operative word and I could sense it in the atmosphere.

On April 23,1975 I informed our staff that the following morning would be our final departure from South Vietnam. Up to this point, no one knew how or when we would be evacuating. As I spoke those words to our staff, I could have heard a pin drop; there was a deafening silence, and no one said a word. The look on their faces is difficult to describe. They were stunned and appeared to drift off into a mild level of shock and disbelief. I began to explain the details of how we would continue to the airport the following morning.

I told them that the flight would leave at full capacity and that we would possibly be leaving in excess of capacity. A decision would be made in the morning whether we would operate a second 747. Why a second plane? Because I wasn't certain we would get everyone onboard. Up to this point we were receiving literally hundreds of requests for passage on our scheduled flights, primarily from Vietnamese women. They had given birth to children fathered by American servicemen who were now back in the United States. The orphan evacuation issue was now reaching chaotic levels. That situation, compounded by the C5-A crash, suddenly became a top priority; decisions and related plans had reached the Oval Office in Washington DC.

A few days prior to our final departure Dan Hood, a Pan Am pilot, arrived on the scene in an effort to evacuate some Vietnamese children for an adoptive family in the United States. Dan was a high school friend of Dr. Jim Simpson and was seeking Dr. Simpson's help to get the children out on Pan Am. Dr. Simpson was a surgeon from California and was in town to help out at the Seventh Day Adventist Hospital. Indeed the hospital had their hands full and needed medical assistance and support. I did not spend too much time with Dan because, at this point, I was dealing with a number of issues that involved hundreds of lives and scheduling operational matters. My message to Dan was simply, "If you can get your seven Vietnamese to the airplane, we will take them."

The number of reservations on the books for our final departure was exceeding one thousand. The bookings were being made in anticipation of tickets that would be transmitted by wire to the Pan Am sales office in Saigon from the United States. Sadly, the tickets were far and few between and the expectations of hundreds of potential passengers were not fulfilled.

I also told our staff that no one would be allowed to take any checked baggage. Whatever personal effects they were planning to take must be in a carry-on bag that could fit under their seat or in the overhead compartment. This was an order that was painful but absolutely necessary. One can only imagine what it would be like leaving your country after living there your entire life and your only personal possessions were what you could cram into a carry-on bag.

Now that all the required documentation to leave Vietnam was completed, I was praying that we would have no problems at the airport checkpoint in the morning. I had all of the approved documentation for everyone and would meet the buses at the checkpoint entry gate at the airport in the morning. On their last night in Vietnam a number of our employees and their families spent the night in the back offices of the downtown sales office. Some slept on the second floor in our accounting office and at the airport offices as well. With the help of the Embassy we arranged for buses to be at the office, at 9:30 on the morning of April 24th.

The procedures for loading this final flight to accommodate an over capacity situation was transmitted to me from Operations Control in New York. This procedure for the evacuation mission was, in a word, unprecedented. It was something the likes of which I had never seen before and never saw again during my twenty-two years with Pan Am. The loading procedure read as follows:

"HEREWITH APPROVED PROCEDURES FOR PASSENGER CARRIAGE ON EVACUATION MISSIONS, NOTE ALL FAA / FAR PASSENGER REQUIREMENTS ARE WAIVED,

ONE / FICL SEATS 2 PASSENGERS PER DOUBLE SEAT, 1 PASSENGER ON FLOOR BETWEEN EACH ROW / BACK TO WALL FEET TO AISLE / REMAINING PASSENGERS ON FLOOR WHERE SPACE AVAILABLE STOP

TWO / ECONOMY AREA, 10 ABREAST CONFIGURATION INCREASE EY *PAX BY 10 PCT,

3 PAX PER TRIPLE SEAT

3 PAX PER DOUBLE / RETRACT ARM RESTS

5 PAX ABREAST IN CENTER SECTION OF SEATS / RETRACT ARMRESTS

THREE / LOAD 23 PAXS IN UPPER LOUNGE, AFTER ALL SEATS OCCUPIED

REMAINDER OF PAX ON FLOOR

FOUR / MAXIMUM NUMBER OF PASSENGERS BASED ON ABOVE PROCEDURES AND USING CONFIG 30 / 370 IS 496 PASSENGERS STOP

FIVE / BASIC LIMITATIONS, OBSERVE NORMAL WEIGHT AND BALANCE LIMITS, SEAT BELT REQUIREMENTS ARE WAIVED, EMERGENCY REQUIREMENTS ARE WAIVED, EMERGENCY EQUIPMENT REQUIREMENTS ARE WAIVED, DO NOT ADD LIFE VESTS/LIFE RAFTS/OXYGEN FOR ADDITIONAL PAX, NO LIMITATIONS FOR INFANTS IN ARMS OR SMALL CHILDREN IN LAPS,

SIX / ALL ABOVE WITH CONCURRENCE OF CREW AND EVACUEES STOP"

After carefully reading the message, over and over again, I became concerned. I was afraid. I prayed. What could be looming ahead was the possibility of an inflight incident that could result in serious injuries. We had insufficient life vests, a serious shortage of oxygen masks and last, but not least, a significant number of people without seatbelts. Our flight plan from Saigon to the Clark Air Force Base in the Philippines was going to be about three hours, a short hop across the South China Sea; but that would be more than enough time to encounter a variety of emergency situations. I was very worried, but I was certain that our staff was concerned only about one thing: when and how do we leave?

As we got closer to those final hours, the United States Air Force was continuing to operate flights to and from Saigon around the clock. The C-141 transport jets were unloading military supplies on the tarmac at the airport. The hardware being dropped off seemed to be rifles, ammunitions, flak jackets, helmets, and an occasional jeep or two. All of this material to help the South Vietnamese army hold off the communist troops.

The South Vietnamese troops were beginning to blend in with the civilian population. They appeared to have absolutely no interest in retrieving the hardware dumped on the tarmac at Tan Son Nhut by the United States. The irony of this last-ditch effort was that we were in effect providing military hardware to the North Vietnamese forces. What was left of the South Vietnamese forces had made their way back to the Saigon area, and they too were looking for a means of escape.

The night before our evacuation flight I did a lot of praying. I could not sleep and so I was up all night. I poured over my checklist of what was supposed to happen in the morning. I was trying to come up with viable options while thinking about all the what ifs. This was serious business. It felt as if we were about to enter a mine field in the middle of the night. Hundreds of lives were at stake. In just a matter of a few short hours we would have a $25 million dollar aircraft heading into a very hostile environment with an all-volunteer crew. Our plan had to work. Our final manifest was inflated and suspect, to say the least. At that time, frankly, I did not know what our final passenger count would be. I received approval to have a second 747 on standby in Bangkok in case we could not accommodate everyone on the first airplane. On paper, with the inflated reservations issues we were dealing with, we had over a thousand people booked on this one flight. I told New York Operations Control that they would be notified as soon as possible if the standby airplane would be needed. But under no conditions should the second airplane be dispatched to Saigon unless I made the call.

On the morning of April 24, 1975, I called the downtown sales office to find out how things were going. I knew that the buses would be there at about 9:30. I was informed that the office was packed with people and I could hear very chaotic noise in the background. As we were speaking, the sales manager told me that the buses had just arrived but that the office was full of customers. He asked, "How do I get them out? What do I tell them?" This was a problem.

I was at the airport and had no intention of heading downtown. The streets were clogged, and Saigon traffic was a mess. We had a 747 heading to Saigon that was one hour away from landing. I was not about to run the risk of being trapped in gridlock and chaos with our aircraft on the ground at Tan Son Nhut. I told our sales manager to inform all of our customers in the office that we were closing early today, and to do whatever he needed to do to clear the office, lock the doors and place a sign on the front door saying, "The Pan Am Office is Temporarily Closed." Then we were disconnected.

Those were the days before cell phones and text messages. Communications were carried out the old fashion way. Dial a number on a rotary phone and hope that you had a line that would remain operational until your conversation was complete. I finally received word that the buses left the downtown office and they were on their way to the airport. To this day I don't know what was done to the clear out the mob that was in the downtown sales office.

Once the buses were en route to the airport, I went to the entry checkpoint to meet them. I was armed with hope, prayer, and several pounds of departure documents. It was a ground zero moment. All of the adoption paperwork was officially signed, sealed, and signed off by the Foreign Ministry. My concern at this critical stage was that the troops at the checkpoint would not recognize the documents as valid and approved by the South Vietnamese Government. The three buses pulled up to the checkpoint. A couple of troops boarded the first bus and I was right behind them. As we slowly walked down the aisle the expressions on the faces of our staff were beyond description; not to mention the increased tension caused by the very visible M-16 rifles the troops were carrying. I'm sure that some of the thoughts going through their minds were, "Have we come this far and this close to freedom to be told that we cannot leave, that we must return to our homes and cannot leave our country?" As the troops completed their inspection, I presented them with the departure documents. They took a cursory look and waved all three buses through.

The three buses proceeded onto the tarmac, directly to the airplane and our employees and some members of their immediate families began the boarding process. This was such a sad moment because we could not be responsible for evacuating every family member for every employee.

Chapter 11
Final Flight Plan / Cleared for Takeoff

Clipper Unity N653PA was now loaded for takeoff. We had almost 500 people onboard the airplane. People were on the floor, in the aisles, in the lavatories and, due to the typical small frames of the Vietnamese people, it was not a problem for some to be two in a seat. Obviously, this was not even close to a basic, routine departure. To begin with, it was a minor miracle that approval to operate the flight from Saigon to the Philippines was finally granted.

In preparation for the final departure, a number of issues had to be resolved. Our Human Resources Director for the Pacific Division, Willard Knapp, spent a few days in Saigon helping me with the administrative details for processing our employees and their families. There was much that needed to be done. We were entering into uncharted waters. It was the first time the company had approved to formally adopt all of their local employees at a Pan Am location, as well as some members of their immediate families. Based on the assumption that we would successfully evacuate everyone to the United States, what was the plan for resettlement, employment, temporary housing, and proper financial support? Secondly, I'll be forever grateful for our Pan Am director in Guam, Ken Sitton, and his staff. Ken was planning for temporary housing for our Saigon employees as soon as they were processed through the refugee facility.

As we began to taxi out to the end of the runway, I finally ended up in the jump-seat behind Captain Berg. Prior to entering the cockpit I walked through the main cabin to determine how everyone was coping. It was a sad walk-through. People were crying; there were forlorn expressions everywhere. Also on board were people that just got on at the last minute. Some of them were relatives of local government officials, and after ditching their uniforms, a few South Vietnamese troops came onboard. As our Regional Security Manager, Cal Yuen, went through the cabin, he collected a few pistols which we confiscated and secured in the cockpit. I did see a couple of the side arms under their shirts as the troops, who had changed into civilian clothing, clambered aboard at the last minute. At that point I made the decision not to intercept them because it could have caused a disruptive, chaotic situation. It was not the time to jeopardize the operation of our final departure from Vietnam. I also realized their situation and understood that they were seeking refuge like the rest of the population. The memories of what happened to the World Airways 727 departure from Danang was still very fresh in my mind. Furthermore I was not too concerned about any possibility of a hijacking, simply because their goal was the same as ours—freedom.

All of us were onboard, doors locked, and the passenger steps pulled back. Our maintenance manager, Jerry Fedorak was on the headset by the nose wheel and gave the order to start engines. With engine starts completed, Jerry climbed up the entry door behind the nose wheel and emerged via what was commonly known as the "Lower 41." His entry into the cabin was through a trap door located in the floor of the forward section of the First-Class cabin.

As we taxied out to the end of the runway, my heart was pounding like a drum. And I do mean pounding. The longer we waited for takeoff clearance, the heavier the heartbeat. Finally, we began our takeoff roll. During that roll I took one final look at our facilities and equipment at Tan Son Nhut Airport, and the hundreds of civilians crowded around the terminal area watching as our beautiful overloaded 747 was on its way to freedom. As we rumbled down, what seemed to be the longest runway ever, I was holding my breath and fully expecting something bad to happen. It never did, and with the nose up and a semi steep climbout, we were on our way. There was just one more hurdle: clear the coastline and head east over the South China Sea.

Seated in the jump seat, behind Captain Berg, I could clearly see the coastline of South Vietnam fading away as we continued our climb and headed for Clark Airbase in the Philippines. Below, I could see several US Navy ships in position for the eminent evacuation of South Vietnam. Once we reached our cruising altitude, I walked through the cabin again to see how everyone was coping with what had just happened. It was a sad moment. There were many tears, expressions of fear and sadness on their faces. Eyes glazed over. Understandably, their mood was somber, mixed with hope about how their lives, in just a matter of hours, would never be the same again.

Some three hours later we touched down at Clark, the US Airbase in the Philippines. When we landed at Clark Air Base, we were required to offload about three-hundred passengers. This would provide space for our regular passengers waiting at the airport in Manila. Pan Am planned to use an Overseas National DC-8 to fly our staff and their families from Clark Air Force Base to Guam. Initially, when I announced the fact that we needed to offload about three-hundred people, to make room for passengers waiting in Manila, no one moved; everyone just sat there. After a short while, however, when they saw the ONA

DC-8, that would take them to Guam, parked next to us, they began to disembark. As they were disembarking, I announced that their next stop was the United States territory of Guam and the refugee processing would begin. I assured them that our staff in Guam would be on hand to help them through this process and supply temporary housing and support during their transition.

Once arriving at Clark AFB in the Philippines, Air Mission #1965/31 would revert back to PA#842 and continue on to San Francisco via Manila, Guam, and Honolulu.

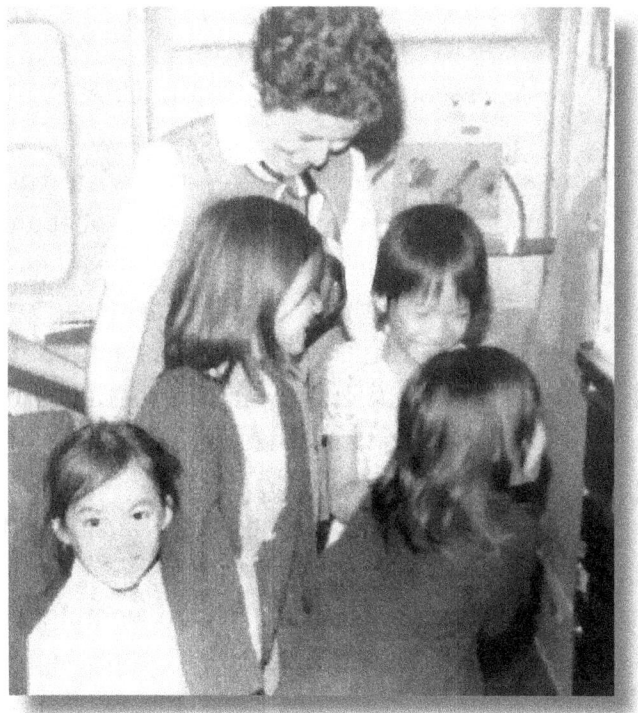

Flight Attendant Laura Lee Gillespie with children of Pan Am Saigon employees prior to final departure from Vietnam, April 24, 1975 (photo courtesy of Flight Attendant Sally Pearl)

Chapter 12
A New Life Begins in Guam, USA

Our staff in Guam, under the supervision of Director Ken Sitton, was fully prepared to meet and handle the arrival of the ONA charter as well as PA#842. I stayed with PA#842 for the short hop from Clark Air Force Base to Manilla before going on to Guam. I settled down into a nice large first-class seat in Manila, took a deep breath and thanked God that we escaped from Saigon unscathed and without incident. So much could have gone wrong during our departure from Saigon, but the Good Lord was definitely working on our behalf and we made it.

Our local boarding passengers began coming aboard in Manila. The flight was running at least four hours behind schedule. A gentleman sat down next to me and asked if I was on the flight out of Saigon. When I told him I was, his next question was, "Do you know why the flight is running so late?" Initially I was somewhat surprised at the question. I thought the entire world was aware of what had just happened, but I asked, "Do you have a few minutes?" As I began to lay out the details of our final departure, he reached into his briefcase and began taking notes. The result of that conversation was a

Saigon employees and families in Guam, April 1975. Will Knapp, Director of Human Resources Pacific Division, second row, second from right. (Author's collection)

story published in the Los Angeles Times twenty-four hours later on April 25, 1975. He was David Lamb, a journalist for the Los Angeles Times. We kept in touch over the years and he attended our thirtieth anniversary reunion on April 24, 2005, in Arlington Virginia.

As soon as we landed in Guam, I was met by Ken Sitton and he briefed me on the details of the plan to process my newly "adopted family" of sixty-one Pan Am employees and their families. The Government in Guam declared that any South Vietnamese refugee, if they could get there by whatever means possible, would find safe haven on the island of Guam. Tents, supplies, volunteers, and United States Government officials were in place to handle and run a refugee processing center on the island.

In advance of the arrival of our Saigon staff, Ken Sitton had secured some temporary housing. A block of rooms at a local motel would serve as their living quarters for an indefinite period of time. The process of registering as legal refugees would allow our staff to seek employment anywhere in the United States. Once finished with this process, Ken was able to offer employment in Guam to a limited number of our Saigon employees. It was a timely opportunity for those hired to work at our station in Guam. Those hired could begin working at once because they were highly qualified. Any additional training would be minimal. As time passed, one of our former Saigon staff eventually married a local Guamanian Pan Am employee. It was indeed a new life in Guam; starting a family and continued Pan Am employment for a few of our Saigon staff.

Several of our other employees had friends or relatives on the US mainland and also in Paris, France. Over the next several weeks and months they moved on to the mainland. Most settled on the West Coast, Texas and the Washington DC and the Northern Virginia areas. Today, Northern Virginia has a significant Vietnamese population and the area is known as Little Saigon, hosting an abundance of Vietnamese shops and restaurants.

Since our final departure from South Vietnam in 1975, we have had two Saigon reunion celebrations. The first was in 1982 and the second was thirty years later in 2005. The 1982 reunion was a complete surprise to me. A number of our former Saigon staff organized the event that was held in Washington, DC. It had been seven years since our evacuation. The seven-year milestone in the Vietnamese culture stands for good luck. At the time I was working in the Pan Am Building in New York City as the Assistant to the Chairman for Consumer Affairs.

In order to keep the secrecy of the reunion, I was invited to attend a special sales meeting in Washington. Jan and I went to Washington and we were totally surprised and appreciative of the outpouring of appreciation and accolades we received. The ladies were all decked out in their traditional Vietnamese dress, the Ao dai. They all looked beautiful as ever. I was also presented with a signed copy of Dr. Henry Kissinger's book, Years of Upheaval, and the Pan Am flag that was once on display next to the American flag in our Saigon Sales Office. After all those years, I still have the flag. It was signed by the staff and, although some of the signatures are now faded, many signatures are not.

The transition from life in Vietnam to life in the United States was traumatic to say the least. Most of our staff lived in Vietnam their entire life. The family members of some employees spoke little, if any, English, which also affected their resettling challenges. Once the preliminary refugee processing was completed in Guam, they moved to the final processing center in Southern California at Camp Pendleton. Life in the camps for the bulk of refugees arriving from Vietnam was difficult. On the other hand, they were free from what would have happened to them had they remained in South Vietnam. During the final days in Vietnam rumors were rampant about the terrible things that would be inflicted on them. There was talk about torture, executions, and re-education camps. For those Vietnamese who worked for American companies and the US Embassy, the treatment would be substantially more brutal.

Fortunately, our staff in Guam had secured motel accommodations, so their first exposure to America was not as intolerable as the temporary accommodations in the tents. It was indeed a new life, a life with an unknown future, but a life of freedom and with hope of a future with unlimited potential. It was a difficult time of adjustment for everyone. They did not know what would happen to their relatives and friends left

Some of the children of Saigon employees after arrival in Guam April 1975 (author's collection)

behind. They did not know if they would ever be able to return to their homeland. They did not know how long the Pan Am support would last. The one thing they did know was that Pan Am would not abandon them and would do everything possible to help them during the emotional transition period. While at Camp Pendleton our Los Angeles employees brought them food, clothing, and other supplies. The outpouring of love and support was remarkable and sincerely appreciated.

Chapter 13
Return to Vietnam Fifteen Years Later

Following the evacuation in April 1975, my Pan Am career continued, with many interesting and challenging assignments. In addition to tours in Okinawa, Osaka, Beijing, and Miami, I worked at the Worldport at JFK as the Manager of the Special Services Department. The Special Services position was challenging, involving the assurance that all of Pan Am VIP passengers received a premier level of service that would be the envy of the industry. The services included greeting VIPs at curbside, escorting them to the Clipper Club and accommodating all the pre-departure needs of CEOs, diplomats and passengers needing wheelchairs.

During the JFK assignment there were occasions when I would escort someone to an aircraft, and I would notice that it was N653PA Clipper Unity (the name was later changed to Pride of The Ocean). Stepping aboard Clipper Unity at JFK immediately brought back vivid memories of our final departure from Saigon. It was always an emotional experience for me. I would walk down the aisle and glance at the faces of three-hundred or more people all settled in for their flight to one of our destinations such as London, Los Angeles, or Paris. They were not the faces I saw back in 1975 and of course none of those passengers had any idea of my personal relationship with that incredibly special airplane. They were looking forward to their trip to Europe or elsewhere and enjoying pre-departure champagne and socializing with their seat mates. The atmosphere had been quite different in 1975; we were over capacity, with almost five-hundred passengers, everyone was sad, many were crying, and there was no pre-departure champagne or pleasantries. Those were times when my thoughts would reflect on those last days in South Vietnam. I would often wonder what happened to the one employee who stayed behind. His decision not to leave was based on family matters. There were nine children in his family at the time and he felt that it would be too difficult to support such a large family in the United States. His elderly mother was not in good health and was more than likely too sick to travel such a great

Return to Vietnam 15 years after the evacuation, October 2, 1990. Met on arrival in Saigon by Luc and his family of 11 children and other relatives.

Return to Vietnam 15 years later. Pan Am logo still over the door of the sales office.

distance by air. The one thing he could not and would not do was leave her behind. I often thought about Luc and hoped that he and his family were doing okay under the new government.

During my special services assignment at JFK our Chairman, Ed Acker, saw me in action one day and offered me the position of Assistant to The Chairman for Consumer Affairs. I suppose that he was impressed with the way I handled a sensitive situation with a customer at the departure gate of our flight to Los Angeles and decided this was the way we needed to handle passenger problems on a regular basis. My primary responsibility was to resolve customer concerns that were addressed to the Chairman and to encourage employees to submit ideas as to how we could improve our operations and provide customers with a consistent level of top-notch customer service. This assignment was, without a doubt, another challenging position in my Pan Am career. Employees around the world were excited about having a direct pipeline to the Chairman's office. I was able to set up communications with several employees from various departments and locations. There were opportunities for travel to stations to see their ideas firsthand, as well as provide an opportunity to recognize some employees for handling unusual situations in an exemplary manner. I also made personal visits and telephone calls to executives to discuss unsatisfactory service experiences encountered during their travel on Pan Am.

It was in 1983 that a letter arrived on my desk on the 46th floor of the Pan Am Building in New York City. The letter was simply addressed to Allan Topping, Pan Am Building, New York, USA. I was stunned when I saw that the return address was from Vietnam and it was from our former employee, Mr. Luc Van Nguyen, who stayed behind in 1975. It was a letter, handwritten in excellent English. As I sat there in the office and read his letter, I was on the verge of tears. He went into some detail about what happened to him and his family after our departure. Once the North Vietnamese took control of South Vietnam, the government did an extensive door to door census on everyone living in South Vietnam. Anyone found to be affiliated in any way with the enemy, that being the United States Government, was enrolled in a "re-education camp." Pan Am was commonly called the official U.S. Flag Carrier. Pan Am played a major role in the Vietnam War. We were a participant in the Civil Reserve Air Fleet Program (CRAF). The program required selected aircraft from US airlines to be committed to support the Department of Defense airlift requirements during emergency situations when the demands of the military fleet was exceeded. Pan Am also operated hundreds of R & R flights for U.S. troops during the height of the war. Those flights went to destinations such as, Hawaii, Australia, Hong Kong, Bangkok, and Taiwan. As far as the North Vietnamese were concerned, if you worked for Pan Am it would be the same as if you worked for the U.S. Government.

Luc's account of life after April 1975 was heartbreaking. He said that he, along with several others, was placed in metal cargo containers located in a remote area on the tarmac at Tan Son Nhut Airport. The conditions were beyond unbearable, as the average outside temperature usually hovered around one-hundred degrees. It is hard to imagine what it was like inside those containers. To add to the suffering, he said that, when an occupant in the container died, the body would remain in the container—sometimes overnight or longer. It was a horrible situation for any human being to endure. He eventually became so ill he was released and sent home to die, but he survived.

In October 1990 I made the decision to return to Vietnam; fifteen years after our final departure. Pan Am was shedding assets at the time due to serious financial issues and we had sold our Pacific routes to United Airlines. It just did not feel the same on a flight across the Pacific on an airline other than Pan Am. Once again, I had several hours to think about all that had happened over the past fifteen years. In a sense, this was another mission of mercy. The US Government had reestablished limited diplomatic relations with Vietnam and the Orderly Departure Program (ODP) was available for those who could qualify. After the war ended in 1975, thousands of Vietnamese continued to flee by boat and ended up on the shores of neighboring countries. The ODP program was created in order to provide a safe and orderly process for them to leave and settle abroad. I was aware of the program and decided to stop at the American Embassy in Bangkok, Thailand prior to flying into Ho Chi Minh City.

The Bangkok stop would accomplish two things; first, I would get the most current information on the ODP Program; secondly, I could share a viewing of the Last Flight Out movie (more about the movie in Chapter 17) with American Embassy staffers and the local press. My mission on this trip was to obtain as much support and information as possible to help me in sponsoring Luc and his family passage to the United States.

While in Bangkok, I learned it was possible that Luc's children, those who were under the age of 21, would be eligible to immigrate to the United States. During the past fifteen years a number of significant changes had taken place in the lives of the Nguyen Family. Sadly, his wife lost her life in a motorbike accident, his mother had passed away, and he now had eleven children. Being a single parent with eleven children is, to say the least, daunting; however, due to the strong family bond in the Vietnamese culture, he was blessed with a wonderful family. His eldest daughter, Le, assumed the motherly role to her siblings during the critical teen years.

Following two days in Bangkok, I boarded the Thai International B-737 for the short ninety-minute flight to Ho Chi Minh City. As I looked at the departure board at the Bangkok International Airport, it seemed odd to note that Saigon was not listed as the destination for my flight. It was simply listed as Ho Chi Minh City (HCM). During the flight to HCM I was reflecting on what took place at that same airport fifteen years earlier. We would soon be touching down on the same runway as well. After we landed and began to taxi to the terminal, I started taking video of the terminal area. It was completely changed. The Ho Chi Minh International Airport was a modern-day airport. As I exited the customs area, I was greeted by the entire Nguyen Family and friends. Immediately, emotional hugs were exchanged, and tears began to flow. It was an emotional moment for all of us. The emotions at that moment were indescribable. It had been fifteen years since

Clipper Unity lifted off Runway 25L fully loaded, leaving Luc and his family behind. We had escaped the eminent takeover of South Vietnam just six days before Saigon fell into the hands of the North Vietnamese troops, but Luc and his family had not.

    During my return visit, I had the opportunity to visit a number of locations that brought back many memories of living and working there in the early seventies. My downtown office walls no longer had the beautifully framed prints of the Pan Am fleet. They had been replaced by a single photo of Ho Chi Minh. Strangely, however, the Pan Am logo remained prominently displayed over the front door of the downtown sales office. I was given the opportunity to visit our residence, which was now occupied by a retired North Vietnamese general. When I went into what used to be my home office, I was shocked to see what was on the desk. It was the American Embassy phone directory that I had left behind fifteen years earlier. The visit was brief. After a cup of tea and some small talk with the family living there, I headed back to the hotel. On the way, my thoughts drifted back fifteen years and I wondered whatever became of our housekeeper. I was never able to find out.

Chapter 14
Last Employee Arrives In The USA

When Clipper Unity left Saigon on April 24, 1975, Luc made the difficult decision, feeling compelled to stay behind. Fortunately, Pan Am was still operating when I began the process of sponsoring him and some members of his family. Under the Orderly Departure Program, only his children under the age of 21 were eligible to immigrate to the United States. During the two-year process of completing the final sponsorship documents, I was successful in raising funds through members of our church (Miami Baptist Church and Wayside Baptist Church) and other fund-raising activities, which would provide temporary support until they settled in and found employment. The funds that were raised covered the air fare from Vietnam to the United States, for Luc and his three youngest daughters. Also, a member of Wayside Baptist Church, Jim Killingsworth, owned a townhouse in Miami and agreed to rent it to the family at a below market price. Our fundraising efforts generated revenues that covered six month's rental upfront. This was indeed a blessing and sincerely appreciated.

On March 27, 1992, almost ten years since receiving Luc's letter, I began tracking their flights from Saigon to Miami. It was a day with a wide range of emotions. As I waited for their arrival, I recalled the day we said goodbye at Tan Son Nhut Airport seventeen years before. Now, it was just a matter of hours before he and his three daughters would arrive in the United States. As they exited the aircraft and entered the terminal, we embraced. It was a night I will never forget.

Arrival of the last employee in Miami, Florida on March 27, 1992. Luc and his three youngest daughters arrive at Miami International Airport. (Photo courtesy of the Miami Herald, used with permission.)

Luc and his three daughters stayed with us for a short while before moving to the townhouse where they would live for several years. Luc's wonderful daughters excelled in school in South Florida and as the time passed, they got married and began raising their families.

Ten years later on April 8, 2002 three more sisters arrived in Miami, Florida. This was another reunion filled with tears of joy. After ten years, the sisters were reunited. Initially the three youngest daughters arrived in 1992 and their sponsorship was approved because they were under the age of twenty-one. Luc's three sons remain in Vietnam and they visit their family members in the US from time to time. Presently Luc divides his time between Florida and Ho Chi Minh City so he can enjoy spending quality time with his children in both countries.

Chapter 15
The Movie - Last Flight Out

Make no mistake, April 1975 was a suspenseful time in South Vietnam. Not only was it suspenseful, it was dangerous. When I reflect on those events of so many years ago, I realize that prayer and the dedication of some special Pan Am flight attendants and pilots played a pivotal role in saving hundreds of lives. I believe it was on the flight from Manila to Guam that I shared this experience with flight attendant, Lisa Yates. A few weeks later, I received a call from John Yates and Norman Cohen. Norman was with Costar Entertainment and John was involved with various Hollywood production companies. They indicated that our evacuation should be made into a movie, or perhaps a book should be written about the experience. My first reaction was that, since there were already so many movies about Vietnam, there was no need for another. They, however, insisted that the last flight out of Saigon was different; it was about ordinary civilians involved in saving lives under extraordinary circumstances during the final days and hours of the Vietnam War. After those first conversations many months passed without any follow up conversations. Actually, I never gave it much thought until I again heard from Norm Cohen. He told me that Michael Manheim, of the Manheim Company, was interested in producing a movie about our last flight out of Vietnam. Michael Manheim is well known for the film, Roe vs Wade. Norm Cohen also said that they were actively seeking a sponsor or sponsors for the film. During the next few years there were infrequent calls from Norm Cohen. He was consistent and positive about seeing the project through; but I was not as optimistic and put it on the back burner.

One day I received a call from Walter Davis. Walter was selected as the screen writer for the movie and he wanted to interview me about Pan Am's final departure from Saigon. That call was a bolt out of the blue. I had given up on a film ever being made, so the phone call was a complete surprise. We set up an appointment for the interview and settled on spending a day in Washington, DC to do the interview.

The interview began in the lobby of the Mayflower Hotel and continued with a walk and a sit-down on a bench in Lafayette Park. It went on for seven or eight hours. As the interview progressed that day, so many memories came back to life.

The film featured four primary characters. First there was Tra, one of our Vietnamese flight attendants who was trying to get her family out before it was too late. She flew in and out of Saigon a number of times prior to our final departure to assist her family in processing the required exit documents. She was portrayed in the film by Rosalind Chao.

Eric Bogosian portrayed Larry Rose. He was a composite character representing a US Government official returning to Saigon to aid in evacuating Vietnamese citizens who worked for the American Embassy in South Vietnam.

Richard Crenna portrayed former Pan Am pilot, Dan Hood. Dan arrived in Saigon just a few days before our final departure to rescue seven people. There were four children; a 22-year-old nurse and her 10-year-old son, and a middle-aged woman and her 17-year-old daughter. The nurse worked at the Seventh Day Adventist Hospital in Saigon.

I was immensely proud to be portrayed by James Earl Jones. He successfully acted out my frustrations as I dealt with a number of difficult issues during the final weeks and days leading up to the evacuation.

Jim Eckes was the general manager for Continental Air Services in Saigon, portrayed by Arliss Howard. During the early days of my Vietnam assignment Jim's friendship was key. He had been stationed in Saigon for a number of years and his knowledge of the local political environment was extremely helpful as I settled in as the Pan Am representative. Our friendship was clearly apparent in the film.

We will be forever thankful to everyone who played a part in this dramatic rescue. Clipper Unity N653PA (the name was later changed to Clipper Pride of the Ocean) was without a doubt, my favorite airplane. I flew on it several times after April 1975. Each time, as I walked onboard, I would gently tap the entry door, whispering to myself, "Thank you." The movie, Last Flight Out, aired on the NBC-TV Network on May 22, 1990.

Chapter 16
Saigon Station Closes

On April 25, 1975, the following message was transmitted to all Pan Am offices worldwide:

PAN AM OFFICIALLY CLOSED DOWN IT'S SAIGON OPERATIONS TODAY AND EVACUATED ALL IT'S EMPLOYEES THEIR DEPENDENTS TO GUAM. THIS ACTION CAME AFTER DAYS OF PLANNING IN NEW YORK AND WASHINGTON AND DIRECTLY FOLLOWED THE US FEDERAL AVIATION ADMINISTRATIONS ANNOUNCEMENT THAT IT WAS SUSPENDING ALL OPERATIONS TO VIETNAM BY US CIVIL AIR CARRIERS. THE ONLY FLIGHTS PERMITTED TO LAND AT SAIGON TAN SON NHUT AIRPORT WERE THOSE AIRCRAFT UNDER CHARTER TO MAC OR THE US STATE DEPARTMENT. THIS MEANT PAN AMS FLIGHTS 841/23 AND 842/24 MANILA/SAIGON/MANILA WERE IMMEDIATELY CANCELED AS SCHEDULED FLIGHTS. HOWEVER THE STATE DEPARTMENT DESIGNATED THE FLIGHTS AS MILITARY CHARTERS AND ....WITH ALL VOLUNTEER CREW HEADED BY SFO / BASED CAPTAIN DAVID BERG. THE 747 FLEW INTO SAIGON TODAY.

THE AIRCRAFT REMAINED ON THE GROUND FOR ABOUT TWO HOURS...WITH SOME CONSIDERABLE SADNESS AND EMOTION...460 PASSENGERS WERE BOARDED INCLUDING 316 PAN AM EMPLOYEES AND THEIR FAMILIES, THE AIRCRAFT FLEW TO CLARK AIR FORCE BASE IN MANILA AND LATER RESUMED IT'S NORMAL SCHEDULE SERVICE AS FLIGHT 842 TO GUAM AND HONOLULU. THE EMPLOYEES AND THEIR FAMILIES TRAVELED TO GUAM ON PA842 ON A MILITARY CHARTER. AL TOPPING ...DIRECTOR FOR SAIGON ...CABLED NEW YORK HEADQUARTERS FROM MANILA THAT ALL PAN AM SAIGON PERSONNEL HAD BEEN EVACUATED AND PRAISED THE MAGNIFICENT EFFORTS OF THE CREW. ANOTHER MESSAGE RECEIVED SAID....ALL SAIGON PERSONNEL ARE DEEPLY GRATEFUL FOR SUCCESSFUL MISSION AND THANKFUL TO BE OUT OF SAIGON JUST PRIOR TO ZERO HOUR. THE ORIGINAL EVACUATION PLAN CALLED FOR A SECOND PAN AM 747 TO FLY TO SAIGON AND THIS WAS STANDING BY IN BANGKOK WITH ANOTHER VOLUNTEER CREW HEADED BY SFO/ BASED CAPTAIN ROBERT BUELTEMAN. HOWEVER THIS FLIGHT WAS CANCELED AFTER THE FIRST HAD CARRIED EVERYONE OUT. THE ONLY PAN AM EQUIPMENT LEFT BEHIND IN SAIGON WERE HEAVY BULKY PIECES...

CAREFUL PLANNING HAD ENABLED MOST PAN AM PROPERTY INCLUDING SPARES TO BE MOVED OUT OF THE COUNTRY IN RECENT WEEKS.

Also left behind were countless memories of a Pan Am operation that touched the lives of hundreds of dedicated employees that worked for an historical aviation pioneer.

Chapter 17
Recollections of Former Pan Am Employees

During the years following the last flight out of Saigon, several of our former Vietnamese employees and other Pan Am employees shared their recollections prior to and after the collapse of South Vietnam. Some of the Vietnamese also shared how their lives changed and described their adjustment to their new life in the US Following are some of their personal and, in some cases, heart-wrenching accounts.

Dr. Helen Davey Former Pan Am Flight Attendant
The R & R Flights
(Source : Pan Am Aviation History Through the Words of Its People, by James Baldwin & Jeff Kriendler)

> *I'll never forget my first glimpse of Vietnam. It was the spring of 1968, after the disastrous Tet Offensive had resulted in an escalation of the war. I was flying my first volunteer flight as a Pan Am stewardess into Saigon to pick up American soldiers and deliver them to their "R*

& R: (rest and recreation) destination. Glued to the airplane window as we approached Tan Son Nhut airport, I was astonished to see actual bomb craters and smoke rising from scattered skirmishes on the ground. I had to give myself a reality check: was this really me, and was I really seeing this, and were American men really being killed right below me? I thought I had seen it all on the nightly newscasts at home, but somehow, I was shocked to see this vision of hell firsthand.

As we taxied around the airport, I felt overwhelmed to see the sheer numbers of war machines of all types buzzing around seemingly everywhere. As we sung the door open, the noise was deafening, and the hot humid air enveloped me, taking my breath away. As I stared out of the open door, I became aware of the pallets of aluminum coffins lined up on the tarmac—each one holding someone's precious husband or son or father or boyfriend or uncle of friend.

I don't think anything could have prepared me for the sight of the soldiers that boarded our airplane. I was expecting to see excited men ready for a new adventure, laughing and joking with each other, and relieved to get away from the war. But as the men quietly filed around the airplane, I clearly saw the faces of trauma. Many were strangely quiet, with expressionless "masks," and most of them stared at our "round eyes" as if trying to take in a bit of home. I had no idea how young these men would be, but I wasn't expecting them to look like they should be in high school! Twenty-five at the time, I wasn't used to being called "Ma'am," and I felt strangely old. I'm convinced that my experiences with these traumatized men helped fuel my later professional interest in the study of trauma.

The Pan Am pilots, mostly ex-military men, felt deep empathy for these soldiers, and their announcements reflected it. And here's where our incredibly talented male purser came in. As funny as any stand-up comedian, he knew exactly how to handle these traumatized men. Totally throwing aside our traditional announcements, he used colorful language that I had never heard uttered on a Pan Am intercom. He spoke right to the men, as if he were waking them up from their nightmare. And he loved to tease the stewardesses! As we were doing our regular emergency demonstrations, we were supposed to point overhead to the forward, center, and aft life rafts in the ceiling. During the part where he was supposed to say, "forward, center, and aft life rafts," he mixed it up and said, "aft, center, and forward." by rote, all of us stewardesses pointed out the rafts in their normal sequence. He said, "So you see, guys, our young ladies don't seem to know their 'forward' from their 'aft!' The soldiers exploded in laughter, and the tone was set for helping to relieve these young men's' burdens for a short time. By the end of the flight, some of the soldiers seemed less robotic, and their eyes were coming alive.

Nothing about the flight felt familiar. Several of the men got up and helped with the serving of meals, leaving us stewardesses with more time to talk to the homesick men. Some of them wanted to ask about what was happening at home, especially about the escalation of protests. One of them asked me to call his mother when I got home, which I did. They showed us pictures of family, children, girlfriends, and wives. They wanted to know all about our crew, where everyone was from "in the world." One Vietnam vet wrote about Pan Am stewardesses that we were "some of the sweetest, caring women I've ever known and need to be recognized for their contribution. Nurse, psychiatrist, mother, sister, daughter, girlfriend, confessor, sex object—they wore all the hats."

So hungry for a touch of home, their eyes pleaded for just a little conversation. I learned on that first flight that if anybody had gone to sleep due to exhaustion, we had to be very careful in waking them up; they would awaken in an extremely startled state, arms flailing, reaching for their imaginary guns. I didn't realize at the time that I was witnessing Post Traumatic Stress Disorder, which might stay with them for the rest of their lives. I picked out one particularly vulnerable looking soldier who's very shy, and as we talked, I decided to become his pen pal. I knew that having a Pan Am stewardess as a pen pal would qualify any soldier as a "rock star."

This was the first of four soldiers that I eventually agreed to have as pen pals. When I began to receive notices, one by one, that each one had been killed, I started to regard myself as a jinx and stopped writing letters. Now I regret this, but at the time it just became too painful for me to be able to put a face to the names of dying men.

Music is where my memory of Vietnam lives, and this time of my life comes with its own special soundtrack; Creedence Clearwater Revival, The Doors, Buffalo Springfield, Jimi Hendrix, Jefferson Airplane, Marvin Gaye, Ike and Tina Turner, Bob Dylan, Crosby Stills & Nash, Otis Redding, The Animals, Aretha Franklin, and Edwin Star who sang "War" ("War! Huh! Good God, y'all! What's it good for? Absolutely nothing!") The music describes wartime—especially the ambivalence about this particular war—better than words can convey. When I hear it, I feel as if were back there. I think that any of us Pan Am employees who flew into Vietnam feel that we, too, were a part of that war. At the time, many of our regular destination cities in Asia were teeming with American soldiers, and wherever there were American soldiers, there was the music, blaring and insistent.

American troops boarding R & R flight in Danang. (photo courtesy of Pan Am Historical Foundation collection)

Willard Knapp
Former Human Resources Director, Pacific Division

The following are some events and experiences that occurred prior to and after the last flight out of Saigon.

I was sent by Ed Swofford (Vice President Pacific Division) to Saigon in early September 1974 to appraise the situation with respect to our employees' safety. Ed had received word from the State Department, via our New York office, that employees of American firms in Saigon were targeted for execution by the North Vietnamese when they captured Saigon. Ed wanted an investigation locally in Saigon to determine if this was just a rumor or, if it seemed likely, to find out what other American firms planned to do. Following my arrival in Saigon, you set up appointments for me with several American firms as well as officials with the military and State Department. As a result of this survey and your input, it became clear that the fall of Saigon was imminent and that we needed a plan to evacuate our employees and their immediate families. Also, plans had to be made to close the station, take out our money, etc. We recommended severance pay for those menial laborers who could not speak English and who would have difficulty coping in America. It is my recollection that our recommendations formed the basis for the eventual plan for the evacuation by a 747 at such time as you gave the signal. On my return from this trip to Saigon, I transited Guam and at that time briefed Ken Sitton (Director-Guam) about the likelihood of our evacuation plans and asked him to look for temporary housing to accommodate our employees and their families. I also asked him to hold open any job vacancies he had, as many of our Saigon employees were professionally qualified.

When we received the signal to fly the 747 for the evacuation from Saigon, I boarded the flight in Honolulu. During the transit of that flight at Guam, I contacted Ken Sitton and told him to get the housing ready as we hoped to bring out the employees on the return flight from Saigon. It was our plan to keep them in Guam until such time as we could get them jobs or get them repatriated back to the US

This proved to be truly fortunate and thanks to Ken's action, we were able to put them into furnished apartments following their arrival in Guam. Following their hectic departure from Saigon, the crowded conditions on the airplane, the uncertainty of their future, as well as the shock of leaving loved ones, they were in a traumatic state when they got off the airplane at Guam. The staff at Guam did a wonderful job during those early morning hours helping them through the clearances at the airport and transporting them to their temporary housing. All the other refugees were crowded in "Tent City" at Anderson Air Force Base.

Many of the employees and families did not fully understand how drastic a change had occurred in their lives. Some thought this was just a temporary situation and that in the not-too-distant future they would be able to return to Saigon and their loved ones who were left behind. They soon began to realize that their future was in the United States and that they might never return. Morale at that point was pretty low. To give them something to think about and take their minds off their problems, we bused them to MacDonald's for a typical American meal—hamburgers, milkshakes, and French fries—the works. At that time, the MacDonald's in Guam was the largest fast-food store in America. This proved a real treat as many had never tasted fast food American style.

Feeding the group was a problem initially. Fortunately, Pan Am had a flight kitchen in

Guam, so we arranged to have meals prepared from our flight kitchen and transported to their temporary housing. That was a difficult logistic problem; but even more troublesome was the fact that this type of food made many of them ill. The drastic change in diet was too much form some to cope with.

Although the private apartments were nice, it was quite a logistic problem as the apartments were not adjacent to each other. Again, thanks to Ken Sitton, some empty cottages were located in a rather remote spot outside of town. There were sufficient accommodations for all the employees and their families. They were furnished very modestly but were adequate. This was a godsend, as we could keep all of the group in one location and families could help and support each other. At that point, thanks to suggestions by some of the wives, we took several of the women on a shopping trip to town. With their help and advice, we purchased pots and pans, utensils, etc., so that they could cook their own food. We then took them to the local supermarket where we bought food, they were accustomed to. From that time on, they cooked their own meals, which prevented any further sickness but also increased their morale, as they were eating food of their choice. It also gave the women something constructive to do, keeping them preoccupied with less chance to worry about their problems.

I learned that many of our Vietnamese were Christians and several were Catholics. On the first Sunday following their arrival, we *arranged bus transportation for all those who wished to attend mass at the Catholic church in town. I went with the group. At the church, prayers of thanksgiving were given, both silent and audible, for the safe trip from Vietnam, as well as prayers for the lives of those left behind. It was a very touching experience and I'm sure it helped many to restore their faith and hope for the future.*

There was an unusual event that occurred shortly after we moved the group into the cottages. I was informed that one of the wives was in labor and about to have a baby. We called an ambulance and got her to the hospital where she gave birth. Many of us went to visit her and found that mother and baby were doing fine. Everyone was delighted that the birth occurred in a US territory. How different it would have been if the baby had been born in Saigon; what a difference a few days meant. It was such a special event that I wired our New York publicity department to include it in our daily newswire that was wired to all Pan Am stations.

There was another dramatic incident which I will always remember because I had a small part in the outcome. The Saigon Maintenance secretary, Diane, an incredibly beautiful young Vietnamese, was in a constant state of depression following her departure from Saigon. She had only recently been married and her husband was in the South Vietnamese military forces fighting the North Vietnamese. She was not able to contact him before her sudden departure from Saigon, so she didn't know where he was after she left. He could have been a prisoner or killed. As a consequence she was understandably in a constant state of anxiety and often in tears. She had no way of knowing if she would ever see him again.

There were certain government officials in Guam who were constantly harassing us to move our Vietnamese to the refugee camp at "Tent City," where the rest of the refugees were. Ken Sitton, through his excellent contacts, was able to placate them. We did commit to them that, at such a time as was necessary to register and process our group, we would bring them to the camp. Sure enough, the request came so we bussed all our employees and their families to the camp. It was a long ordeal and a lot of red tape to get through. Those who were not yet called and those who had finished the processing waited inside the bus. I was in one of the buses, sitting near Diane. Suddenly she stood up and pointed out the window towards a young Vietnamese man. She screamed at him to come over to the bus. She said that from a distance he looked like her husband. I rushed out and grabbed him before he got away and said, "There's someone inside the bus who wants to see you." I took him over to the bus and Diane burst into tears and exclaimed, "It's my husband. He's alive!" Can you imagine the joy, elation, and level of emotion as a result of this wholly unexpected reunion in Guam, in the middle of the Pacific Ocean?

After the emotions subsided somewhat, the husband told how he had been evacuated by the military and brought to Guam with other refugees. He was awaiting evacuation to a camp in the US and was expecting to leave momentarily. This, of course, meant another separation from Diane. There was no telling how long it would take them to find each other after they were sent to the US I told him about our separate housing arrangement and said, "Look, there are about 10,000 Vietnamese here and, since you are already processed, why don't you just get inside the bus with us? I'm sure you will not be missed and this way you can stay with Diane." So he did. We all heaved a sigh of relief when the bus left the camp without further incident. I have often wondered what happened to this young couple after their repatriation to the US

There were exceptions to the fact that all the Vietnamese were repatriated to the US Ken Sitton did keep eleven job openings and we arranged for interviews for those openings for our qualified former Saigon employees. Eleven of them were hired and warmly accepted by the Guam staff. Most of the Vietnamese were excellent workers; intelligent, ambitious, bilingual and achievers. It was amazing how they adapted so quickly. I remember helping one of our Vietnamese operations supervisors get his Guam driver's license. He tried to pass the test three times and each time he failed. It was essential for him to drive a car after he was hired by Pan Am at Guam, because no other transportation was available, and he would also be able to drive some of the other Vietnamese to work. He persisted, however; and in only a couple of weeks following his arrival in Guam, he passed the test and obtained his license.

Pan Am made a wholehearted effort to find suitable jobs in Pan Am for the other employees. We compiled resumes for each employee, which we sent to Personnel in New York. We also posted their qualifications and availability to all Pan Am locations in the US

Looking back on the experience in Guam, I recall that I initially had some misgivings when I was assigned the overall responsibility for seeing that our Vietnamese and their families were housed, fed and sustained in Guam until their eventual evacuation to the US Now, I feel grateful for the opportunity to be able to aid and get to know this special group because they were exceptional under the circumstances. I cannot praise enough the spirit, resourcefulness and adaptability demonstrated by them.

Al, it was a real thrill to have been invited and to participate in the 15th reunion gala. It was one of the most rewarding and emotional experiences in my lifetime. Thank you again.

Sincerely,
Will Knapp

Marilyn Weber Marsden
Coordinator for The Community Action Program (CAP)
(Source: (Source : *Pan Am Aviation History Through the Words of Its People,* by James Baldwin & Jeff Kriendler), by James Baldwin & Jeff Kriendler)

The Vietnam war was responsible for the production of thousands of orphans. Many were cared for in orphanages and several others were cared for in foster homes. It was common knowledge that the North Vietnamese viewed these mixed-race children with great disdain and they fully supported the evacuation of the Amerasian orphans.

In 1974 the Pearl S. Buck Foundation approached Pan Am to take part in a program to provide escorts for orphaned children from Vietnam to the US The escorts would be Pan Am flight attendants. The flight attendants who volunteered to participate in the program would do so on their vacation time. The program was called The Community Action Program.

Marilyn Weber Marsden was selected to be the Coordinator of the program. As coordinator Marilyn's first task was to write the policies and procedures for the escorts. The escorts were given free positive space passes on Pan Am from Saigon to the West Coast of the United States. Since Pan Am did not have domestic flights at that time, an agreement was arranged with United Airlines to provide complimentary travel to interior cities in the US The Foundation paid the expenses for the escorts during the Honolulu layovers and the two days in Saigon. Escorting the orphans on a one-to-one basis was the most expeditious way to get the children to their waiting adoptive parents in the United States. Otherwise it would require a group of children to be approved for adoption before supplying an escort.

Marilyn would make the initial trip to Saigon and escort the first child back to the United States. In addition to her required travel documents she also carried a bag full of antibiotics, compliments of her brother who was a doctor. These medications were for the Friends For All Children orphanage run by Rosemary Taylor, also known as the mother of a thousand children. When Marilyn arrived at the orphanage Rosemary was waiting for her and she said, "I have a sick child upstairs who is dying." And with that Rosemary took the bag of antibiotics and headed upstairs to care for the sick child.

This mission to Vietnam was to escort a 3-year-old Nguyen Thi Thu back to Philadelphia, PA. When Marilyn arrived at the home of the foster parents the foster father greeted her. They talked for a while over tea and by the way he looked at Thu she knew that parting with this 3-year-old was going to be difficult. The next day it was time to say goodbye and the foster father handed her over to Marilyn and the tears in his eyes said it all. He said, "I love you and I will never see you again. I hope you are going to a loving family and that you will have a better life."

The flight from Saigon to Philadelphia would include spending one night in Honolulu, Hawaii. During the stopover in Honolulu another CAP volunteer greeted them warmly and spoke to Thu in her native language. It was a long trip from Honolulu to Philadelphia and her adoptive parents met them on arrival at the Philadelphia International Airport. Thu was adopted by Nancy Kalan and her husband Chuck who had two children of their own. Thu was the first Vietnamese child brought into the United States for adoption under the auspices of the Pearl Buck Foundation. Now her name is Trista Joy Kalan.

There's one more piece to this wonderful story. Thu had a brother in foster care in Vietnam and she missed him terribly. Thu was assured that she would be reunited with her brother as soon as his paperwork could be completed and approved. Two months later her two-year-old brother arrived in the United States and was adopted by Nancy's sister Mille-Jean Corliss who lived nearby in Richboro, PA.

The Last Flight out of Saigon
Former Flight Attendant- Laura Lee Gillespie

The evacuation of Pan Am's employees and their families out of Saigon on April 24, 1975 was a dramatic event.

Our Captain, Bob Berg, volunteered his service as did the rest of the cockpit crew, flight service crew and the orchestration of the evacuation by Al Topping, Station Manager, Saigon. Al Topping had an enormous responsibility towards the employees and their families. Al knew that the airport was going to be shut down but he didn't know what day and he had to choose the best time for the evacuation and make sure that all the people were in place for this rescue mission. It was a tremendous effort.

I was in Tokyo and received a call from Pan Am Operation's in the middle of the night. They asked if I would volunteer to go into Saigon on a rescue mission. I said yes. They sent a crew bus to pick me up. We went from Tokyo to Manila, about four hours flight time, and picked up the rest of the flight service crew— Sioux Matson, Pamela Taylor, Tra Duong and Gudrun Meisner.

They had been waiting in Manila for several days—ready to go. Apparently the first rescue aircraft assigned to go into Saigon was cancelled and they had to wait for our plane.

Captain Berg briefed the crew and hands me the order FAA issued that all passenger carriage requirements were waived—seat belts—emergency equipment, etc. Captain Berg also briefed the crew about a limited time factor and said he would flash the

red beacon light if any trouble arose on the runway. He said, "If the beacon light flashes you better head for the aircraft because that means we have to leave."

When we landed in Saigon and walked through the terminal, I saw a mass of people outside the gates trying to get into the airport. The gates were shut, and they were screaming and crying "take my baby," "take my children." They pleaded with us to take their babies. It was a very distressing sight.

The memory of passengers squeezed together on seats, sitting on the floor between seats, small children, and babies on laps. We tried to keep the isles clear so we could walk through the cabin. The upper lounge overflowing with passengers, including Tra Duong's four sisters she was able to get through immigration wearing Pan Am uniforms collected in Manila by crew members. Everyone was so sad and yet so grateful and thankful to be leaving the impossible situation that had built up in Vietnam.

The flight service crew on this flight represented Pan Am in an exemplary manner with their willingness to sacrifice time and effort for the welfare of the evacuation.

Sometime after the evacuation I received a call from Captain Berg. He left a recording on my answering machine. I felt I had to transcribe this recording to send to my crew so they would know what Bob had to say.

"Laura Lee, this is Bob Berg and I'm calling to thank you for my pictures and for the chance to see you again. I have a feeling—I've many times thought—that you people were not truly aware of the actual danger that you were in the whole while. In fact when I left Manila, I took just enough fuel to go back to Saigon and back to Manila. When we got to Manila, they wouldn't let us land so we went up to Clark and I got enough fuel to get to Manila plus 45 minutes where it was just enough to get back to Clark. So we landed with 15 minutes left of gas and I didn't bother to tell you *people because I figured you'd be worried. It was a dangerous mission and I was so extremely proud of all of you for volunteering and going along with that. Anyway I appreciate your pictures very much. Thanks a lot. Bye Bye."*

Former Saigon Sales Agent, BN

It is still deeply painful to look back, yet I recall it so clearly. It was April of 1975 when I nervously boarded a US Embassy bus, my two young children and a small suitcase in tow, that was to covertly transport us and other desperate Pan Am employees and their families to Tan Son Nhut Airport in Saigon. It was a tangled whirlwind of sadness, hope, fear, and anticipation. In the hours before the escape attempt, I had to say goodbye hurriedly and tearfully to my youngest brother who had just narrowly escaped from a town in central Vietnam just a few days earlier, right before it fell to communist occupation. I was told that I had to leave him behind, as only immediate family members would be allowed on the flight. I handed him an envelope which held my last paycheck and instructed him to search for the rest of our family who lived 300 kilometers away outside of Saigon. I had heard no news from my mother, nor my sisters, and wasn't certain whether they were safe, or whether they were even alive. Leaving my beloved family behind was heart-wrenching. The only sure thing I knew was that my future was uncertain, and that I must get out of Vietnam before it fell.

Words do not describe the profound sadness, fear, and anxiety that I felt, that indeed we were all feeling.

The bus jetted us down the tarmac directly to the Pan Am Flight 842. Everyone's eyes were fixed on it like a symbol of promise and strength. Crossing the tarmac seemed like crossing oceans, taking me farther and farther away from my beloved country. We hurried onto the plane, and after a tense negotiation between the brave volunteer Pan Am staff and airport security, I could hear the aircraft door finally latched close, ending a chapter in all of our lives. A voice from the cockpit reassured us and announced that Flight 842 was ready to leave, and approximately 30 minutes later, the captain announced that we had reached international airspace. That moment, that voice, and those words, are embedded in my heart forever. I realized at that moment that I was leaving behind my mom, my brothers, my sisters, and saying goodbye to my Vietnam. I didn't know when I would see either again.

I looked around. People's eyes were flooded with tears of joy and tears of loss. The fear of our plane being brought down by North Vietnamese was replaced with fear of an uncertain future in a new foreign land. With no relatives, no job, and nowhere to go, all I could cling to were my suitcase, my children, and my memories. When we arrived in Guam, I was extremely grateful to be rehired by Pan Am and worked there for two and half years before moving to Washington DC, where I stayed with Pan Am until 1986.

Al, when you asked me to write a few lines for your book, the first thing that came to my mind was to say, "Thank you." Thank you for all your laborious and heroic efforts to get your Pan Am employees and their families to safety. Thank you for not leaving us. Thank you for staying and risking it all to save us. I will be saying thank you to you in my heart for the rest of my life. You were forced to make difficult life or death decisions during the days, and even the minutes that led up to this dangerous mission. Some of the decisions you had to make must have been gut-wrenching, yet you made them and led us all to safety.

Recollections of Lien Ta,
Former Customer Service Agent, Tan Son Nhut Airport

When I left for work on April 24, I was determined, but also nervous and anxious. I was determined because I was convinced that leaving Vietnam was absolutely necessary. But I was also apprehensive because I knew that I was leaving behind all that was familiar and comfortable. I had no clear idea of what lay ahead for my family and I as we and nearly 500 others left Ton Son Nhut Airport on Pan Am's Last Flight Out.

If there was a hero in this story, it was Al Topping, my boss. He did what a true leader does. He refused opportunities to leave Vietnam for safer ground until all his people and their immediate families could leave with him. He planned the events of that last day, ensured everyone had the proper documents, and left with the rest of us. It was an extraordinary act of courage that has been memorialized in a feature film and most recently highlighted at an October 26, 2019 gala event at the Pan Am Museum in New York City. I and five other former Saigon employees were honored to attend the event recognizing once again Mr. Topping's heroic efforts.

In my own case, the process of adjusting to new surroundings and a new culture was helped a great deal by what happened in Guam, the destination point for our last flight out of Saigon. The local Pan Am team in Guam welcomed and greatly aided the entire Pan Am contingent. My great fortune personally was that I was chosen to be among those who immediately began working for Pan Am in Guam. In a matter of two days, I went from doing my job in Saigon to essentially doing the same job in Guam.

The two years that I worked in Guam helped a great deal with my transition to a new way of life. The familiar work environment and supportive co-workers both helped make easier not only the immediate transition, but also the eventual transition to life in the United States.

Finally, the adjustment to life in the US was helped by the existence of a large group of family and friends spread across the country who were able to support one another while putting down new roots.

Lien (Linda) Ta work history with Pan Am:

1967-75 – Tan Son Nhut Airport, Saigon
1975-77 – Guam International Airport
1977-90 – Washington Dulles Airport, Washington, D.C.

Recollections of Diana Nguyen, Former Secretary, Maintenance Department, Tan Son Nhut Airport, Saigon

Your letter dated May 30, 1990 has been received some time ago, and you know what? You were right when you said that I must have lots to write about but each time I tried to put it in writing, my head just went blank. I wish I were an eloquent writer to be able to express my feelings thoroughly.

Thank you for asking me to participate with you in this long overdue venture. However, I don't know where to start, even though the memory is always fresh in our mind. Often, my husband and I do reminisce with our friends about what had happened in those final days. It has been 15 years now and the pain comes and go but the events will never be forgotten!!

We all have been struggled to make a living and try to adjust ourselves with this total new life, language, culture, and traditions, but thanks to the grace of God combining with luck we manage to keep our heads above the water and overcome with everyday difficulties as well us obstacles. We are now employed and the kids are doing well in school: one already on his own, the two boys that you met at the party, Peter is in college and Stephen is a tenth grader at Rolling Hills High School.

There is not much I can tell you more about our evacuation on that historic day than you already knew except I was terrified, scared, and more like a walking zombie when I was told by Jerry Fedorak that for my safety he suggested that I should leave the next day because Flight 842/24 April 1975 will be our last flight out of Saigon. So that evening I came home and briefed my husband about the conversation with Jerry. As a high-ranking officer, my husband was aware of the hopeless situation; he knew that only a miracle would be able to save South Vietnam but he still decided to stay behind with his men and agreed to let me pack a couple Pan Am's bags of clothes, some dried food, and my two sons ages 7 and 4 for a journey to an unknown destination. He told me that at least if something happened to him, he still be content that somewhere in the new world his children are safe.

My Mother accompanied my children and me to the airport as my husband was unable to leave the air base. At first, the order from you was that each employee can only bring their immediate family and so I made sure to abide with this rule and left my poor mother behind the gate but later I found out other people had brought along their entire family and some with distant relatives made me realize how naive I was and frankly, I still live to regret until today that I didn't take chances like other people, but come to think of it nobody could do anything better on that horrified exodus.

When Pan Am B747 was released after hours under the sizzling sun, we reached Clark Air Force Base in the Philippines and due to the weight of the aircraft you decided to separate us into two groups and offloaded half of the passengers onboard for the next available flight to Guam. When we arrived at Guam the next day, it was like a nightmare for me to suddenly realize in one day I have lost everything; my privileged life, my house, family, relatives, and friends and now stranded in an abandoned Navy camp, homeless, jobless, and penniless. At that time, if it weren't for my children, I probably would have committed suicide! There seems nothing left for me in life. But here comes Mr. Al Topping to the rescue! I found out later that after you have settled in the other half group which accompanied with you on the flight, you next effort was to locate the remaining of the Pan Am employees and chartered a bus to move all of us into comfortable apartments in Guam. I still vividly remember that afternoon when you and Jerry Fedorak took me and my kids out to McDonald for a first taste of Big Mac. Wow!! The food was so good that nothing can compare with it.

On May 1, 1975, when Saigon finally fell into the hands of North Vietnam, my husband escaped with his last crew from Tan Son Nhut Air Base on the DC-6 that was given to President Thieu by Pan Am; he was able to contact with us through Pan Am office in Guam. We stayed in Guam for about two weeks and joined with the other refugee flux to go to California.

We later transported to Camp Pendleton in the freezing night on May 5, 1975, and again surrounded by Marine military men, high fences, and armed guards for about two months. While in the camp, we slept on cots and shared our tent with 15 other people. Because we were not used to the weather, food etc. combining with homesick, we were really miserable and cry a lot. During the time at the compound, Pan Am and their employees in Los Angeles made several trips to visit us. They brought us food, clothes, and other much needed items. That was really nice of them! They were so loving and caring that now while writing the words to you I feel so emotional that my eyes are flooded with tears.

A week after we left Camp Pendleton, Pan Am in Los Angeles offered me a job as a senior secretary. My young new boss accepted me without any doubt of my four-month pregnancy and my ability to perform the job. My husband was not that lucky. He landed a job as a cleaner of Continental Airlines. Needless to say, he was very sad and depressed at first because he never thought that after years working hard in schools and years in the Vietnamese Air Force serving as a pilot, pilot trainer, and squadron commander, he ended up working in this extremely "entry level" job but gradually we've come to realize that ups and downs are just part of life; he is not the only one to have started off in America with industrial jobs. We *were lucky to be alive and the most important thing is that we still have each other and the freedom that we might not have if we had not left our homeland.*

Pan Am laid me off in July 1985 after a strike by TWU union workers. I now work for Rockwell Int'l as a Plan/Schedule Analyst, and my husband after a few layoffs with different companies, spent a few years in Technical College. Currently he is working as an aircraft inspector for American Airlines.

Yes, America is a rich and beautiful country. I will not stop this letter without saying thank you to her and her people for opening their warm welcome arms to our people and giving us the chance to live in freedom and full of opportunities. However, my heart never stops aching every time I think of my small and war-torn country, even though Vietnam is rated as one of the world's poorest countries. I still love Vietnam with its beautiful while sandy beaches, lovely tree-lines streets, gorgeous countryside with long and green rice paddies. Well, the truth is people never know how much they miss anything until it's not around anymore.

It's always been my dream that one day I might have a chance to go home safely to visit my aging mother and my father's grave (he died shortly after I left), to hug and talk to my brothers, sisters, nieces, and nephews that I have not seen in the long 15 years. But until then, I will wait.

Love, Diana Nguyen

P.S. Thank you for reading this letter. My intention is just to share a few memoirs and my deep thoughts with you. I have no desire to go beyond this. Please keep in touch and send my regards to Jerry if you happen to see him.

Recollections of Flight Attendant Karen Walker Ryan's Operation Babylift Experience
(Source: *Pan Am Aviation History Through the Words of Its People*, by James Baldwin & Jeff Kriendler)

We arrived in Hong Kong from New Deli and the next day we were going to head to L.A. via Tokyo, with one last night in Tokyo and we would be home the next day. We got on the bus in Hong Kong to go to our hotel. Then someone came aboard and told us there was a telegram from the home office. Flights home were canceled for the following day and we were being rerouted to Saigon and we would be evacuating babies. It was explained to us that, "We have something like 300 babies and about 150 children between the ages of two and twelve. We have a few volunteers going along to help with the kids. That's what you will be doing." So we went to the hotel. I don't remember the option of being a volunteer, but I understand later that a couple of gals called the home office and said, "I can't do this; I'm going home," and they didn't have to go. But I was young and invincible; I didn't care, I was going. But then we got to the hotel, we looked at the TV in the lobby that had all this footage of the C5-A, which is an Air Force big cargo plane that had just crashed in Saigon; and it was full of babies that were going to the States, and half the babies died. We didn't know much else—just that a plane full of babies had crashed. We didn't know if it had been shot down, we didn't know anything. So we were nervous. We already knew that Danang had fallen. We had already seen all of the footage at home of people hanging onto airplanes trying to get out of Danang, the civilians. So we knew that it was quickly falling all over the country.

So we slept that night, got up early the next morning, and got on a spotless 747. We had cardboard bassinets that we had to assemble, we had closets full of milk bottles that we had to fill with formula and mix with water; we were getting the giant 747 ready for all the babies.

We get to Saigon and the pilot just aimed for the runway, making a sharp descent and I could not believe he could make a 747 do that—just in case we were going to take fire—and we landed. We taxied by the burned shell of the C5A that was still smoking. We parked at a far corner on the tarmac, way far away from the terminal and we waited, it was nice and cool in our jet and we had everything ready to go, and then came all these rickety buses full of all these babies and we opened the door of our cabin to the tropical air and here comes people, up the stairs, holding babies, one under each arm, handing them to us and then they would *go back down the stairs and we take the babies and get them into the bassinets and we go back to the door and get more babies, and more, and they just kept bringing these babies, and we just kept taking them and it seemed it would never stop. In my mind I was thinking, "Where are the mothers, where are the mothers?" It was a jolt as to what war does—it went on and on and on. We filled all the bassinets; we would put two babies in a bassinet, and then we would put two or three babies under a single seatbelt. We had babies in seats and on the floor where your feet should go, under the seat. I had been so sheltered; I had never seen a baby with a cleft pallet, or babies who were so ill and emaciated. A lot of them looked good, but a lot of them were ill. So we had to figure out who was really deathly ill and get them up to the first-class cabin which we had turned into a triage where our doctors had set up IV's.*

Then came the older kids and that was just as traumatic. Some were on crutches, all of them crying and everyone was a complete emotional wreck and the babies were all howling. Finally, we got everyone on board and—as I understand, we took a lot more than they said we were going to take—thanks to our station manager, he smuggled aboard a lot of his Vietnamese crew and their families as well. The South Vietnamese, to the very end required that every I had to be dotted, every t crossed on their paperwork. They needed all this paperwork. The way I understand it is that everyone who brought the babies onboard just started to make up their own paperwork to satisfy the bureaucracy that was left of the failing government.

We got them all on board, closed the doors, and started up the engines. I remember draping myself over the babies on the floor, as far as I could reach, and other stewardesses were doing the same thing. We took off, straight up and out of there.

Once we got up to cruising altitude, the cabin cooled down, the babies found their thumbs and went to sleep, and we started doing our job. We went around and started checking babies to make sure they were still breathing. We had a lot of babies to check. We served hamburgers to the older kids. It was odd because I had never served hamburgers on Pan Am before. We had about three big barrels of clothing, so when a baby would soil its clothes, we would grab something that we thought would fit and were constantly changing clothes, putting diapers on; a lot of them had diarrhea.

Before we knew it, we were coming into Guam and that was where we were getting off. So we landed in Guam and I understood that plenty of people came aboard to help, volunteers from bases in Guam and a lot of the wives and daughters of military guys. A new crew went on and we went to our hotel and the Operation Baby-lift flight went on to San Francisco.

Recollections of former Purser
Pam Taylor

It was 1965 when my letter of acceptance arrived from Pan American World Airways stating that I was requested to report for training in NY. I was thrilled because I knew I would be able to travel the world. I knew it would be exciting and full of adventure. But I had no idea that I would have a front row seat to many historic and world-changing events. My twenty-five-year career with Pan Am would be filled with such exposures.

One such example was the last flight out of Saigon, which at the time was under attack by the North Vietnamese. This last flight out was perhaps the pinnacle as well as the nadir of all those years of flying. It was an escape under fire, for our crew as well as the fleeing Vietnamese. We were together in this: men, women, and children.

That amazing adventure had its start in April 1975 when Pan Am called me at home to see if I would be willing to take a mercy flight into and out of Saigon. After clearing it with my husband, Tom, I called Pan Am back and accepted the assignment. Almost immediately, I was on my way to what would become a two-week adventure full of fear, unspeakable sadness, exhilaration, and accomplishment.

At home during the last few months, local media had been full of dire warnings regarding the major push of the North Vietnamese and the weakened resistance in the South. It was reported that many cities in the North were throwing down their equipment and fleeing. Panic seemed to be occurring everywhere.

Our volunteer crew was positioned in Manila when we heard that our departure for Saigon was imminent. United States President Gerald Ford had telegrammed permission to Pan Am to lift all FAA restrictions. We would be allowed to pack as many evacuees as possible into our plane. Seatbelts were not needed; people could sit on the floor and between aisles; no baggage was to be taken on board so we could board the maximum number of people that the plane could lift.

After landing in Saigon, Captain Berg told us that he would not leave anyone behind — and that the signal for immediate departure would be the red flashing light on top of our 747. Once the light was flashing, we were to return to the aircraft immediately. But getting non-uniformed people onto the aircraft ran into a major last-minute obstacle. South Vietnamese with guns were demanding visas to allow passengers to board the plane. Greed was on full display, but since they were armed, we began to collect South Vietnamese currency from the few passengers who had managed to get on board because they had the required visas. The crew passed a pillowcase around to collect South-Vietnamese Piasters, especially since they would have no value to the evacuees in their new lives. We quickly rushed the pillowcases with cash to the bottom of the ramp where the refugees were frantically trying to board the aircraft. We had brought in uniforms and wigs so we could smuggle out four of the sisters of one of our flight attendants who happened to be Vietnamese.

I felt an overwhelming compassion for these strangers who were relieved to be escaping Vietnam but at the same time sad for their loss of country and family left behind. There was a lot of love in our 747 that day! We did not need to talk; passenger hands reached over the aisles to touch my hands. I walked the aisles and tried to comfort them. All of our crew were overwhelmed by the emotions, which ranged from relief to fear to grief.

The plane was racing and about to lift. As I secured my own seatbelt and closed my eyes for a moment, I started to cry. I realized that our passengers were leaving families and friends as well as their country.

For almost twenty years, I could not talk about Pan Am's evacuation flight without sobbing. I remain proud to have worked for Pan Am, a company that did so much good in so many evacuations around the world.

Pan Am on Amber One
By John Krimsky, former Vice President for Government Affairs

Both Pan Am and Air France supplied technical support to Air Vietnam for many years prior to major hostilities and the fall of Saigon in 1975. Air Vietnam had leased a Boeing 727-100 from Pan Am and had expanded its Green Dragon Routes throughout Southeast Asia.

Less than two months after the fall of Saigon in June 1975, one Air Vietnam B-727 was flown from Hong Kong to Vietnam by Chief Pilot Captain Huynh Minh Boong.

Pan Am was unable to help in the return of the other B-727 from Taiwan and was later denied overflight rights using the air route Amber One. This denial of access to Amber One created a significant expense and added flight time between Hong Kong and Bangkok on Pan Am's round-the-world services. It additionally created a severe competitive disadvantage and one that the US Government could not help in resolving as the US had no diplomats in North Vietnam and no relations with Vietnamese legations outside of Vietnam.

It was left to members of the Pan Am management team to intervene and try and contact the government in Hanoi to determine what it would take to allow Pan Am to utilize once again Amber One. After months of camping out near the Vietnamese Embassy in Bangkok, an invitation to visit Hanoi was finally provided.

With the help of a team of Irish aircraft brokers at Shannon, a Boeing 707 was delivered to Vietnam. Air Vietnam ceased to exist, and the 707 and 727 from Hong Kong were the first two aircraft transferred to the new Vietnam Airlines.

With the impending invasion of North Vietnam into the south, Air Vietnam management and crews decided to use the precious days remaining to help South Vietnamese citizens escape to neighboring countries. In the final hours before North Vietnamese troops overran Tan Son Nhut Airport, Air Vietnam planes still able to fly left with their final passenger loads.

Today, Vietnam Airlines boasts a fleet of A350's and A321's making it the largest Airbus fleet in Asia. It has added B-787's and B-777-20 ER's and expects to be the second-largest full-service carrier in Asia in 2020.

Amber One overflight of Viet Nam, Laos, and Cambodia remains an essential part of aviation history and many memories for the Pan Am people involved in its reinstatement.

About the Author

I was born in Montego Bay, Jamaica. My Father, Allan, worked at the Ethel Hart Hotel in Montego Bay. He was the all-around handyman and, among other things, he was a chauffeur and a waiter. He was extremely handy to have around, as he could fix just about anything that wasn't operating properly. I can recall when, while growing up in Brooklyn, he built a radio from scratch through a correspondence course. He could take apart and put together again just about any malfunctioning appliance, and it always seemed as though he did it with a good amount of ease.

My Father immigrated to the United States in 1944 under a sponsorship from one of the regular guests of the hotel where he worked in Montego Bay. A year after serving out the commitment to his sponsor, my mother Gwendolyn, my sister Yvonne and I immigrated to the United States to join him in 1945. The Pan Am ticket office in Kingston was the place to go to secure some of the necessary travel documents. It is interesting to note that the Pan Am ticket office was sort of like an American consulate. They were authorized to provide all the necessary travel documents needed to immigrate to the United States.

During my early childhood years in Jamaica I had some not so typical experiences that I'll always remember. One day I was running around in the yard, barefoot as usual, and stepped on a conch shell, resulting in a deep cut on the left side of my left foot. A bright red fountain of blood shot up in the air and landed on a nearby frog. I ran into the house screaming, "Mama, a frog bit me!" Later, I fainted and, with blood-soaked towels wrapped around my foot, a neighbor carried me to the dispensary about a quarter mile away. We did not have a car, but we sure could have used one that day. The things we normally needed were usually within walking distance. By the way, the scar remains on my foot to this day.

We began our life in the United States in the Bedford-Stuyvesant section of Brooklyn, New York. Bed-Stuy, as it was called, was a typical melting pot community. We lived in a three-story brownstone which my parents purchased in the 1950's for $9,000.00. The Hirsches, a very nice, friendly Jewish family, lived next door. They had two children, Jerry and Shirley. Jerry and I both loved to play baseball, so we played together almost every day and we became very good friends. We played stickball in the street and baseball in nearby Tompkins Park. Further down the block were Puerto Rican families, black families and more Jewish families. Those were wonderful days.

Then things started to change. The neighborhood gangs were becoming a serious problem. As the neighborhood deteriorated the white families were fleeing to the suburbs and leaving only the black and Puerto Rican families as residents. It finally reached the point where my parents saw the need to relocate as well. We moved to the Borough of Queens to a pleasant, quiet suburban community called Hollis.

I am forever thankful to God and to my parents who were devoted Christians. They maintained the strength and courage to raise my sister and me in such a way that we were able to navigate through the challenges of living in the ghetto and emerging unscathed. Bed-Stuy was a tough neighborhood, filled with gangs, gang fights, drugs, robberies, shootings and other unseemly events. I often viewed some of those unfortunate situations from the third-floor window of our brownstone house, where we lived for about ten years. The peer pressure was intense and I was teased a lot in elementary and high school because I could not and would not join a gang. Following my graduation from Boys High, I attended New York City Community College. After only one year I became bored with economics and business administration. I wanted to go to work. So off I went. My first full time job was with the Wolff Book Binding Company on the West Side of Manhattan in New York City. I worked as a clerk in the stock room, and it was hard work. It involved unloading trucks with various material for printing and binding books.

After a couple of years at the book bindery, an opportunity came up to work for the International Institute of Education (IIE). The position was in the travel department and my official title was Transportation Specialist. My primary role involved making travel arrangements for hundreds of foreign students. The students were recipients of grants from a variety of benefactors such as the Ford Foundation, The Rockefeller Foundation, Fulbright Scholarships, and the US State Department. I will go into more detail about my employment with the Institute, United Airlines and Pan Am in Chapters 3 and 4.

We hope you enjoyed Allan H. Topping's account of Pan Am's final flight out of Vietnam. Please be sure to theck the other titles offered by BluewaterPress LLC. They may be found online at www.bluewaterpress.com.

www.ingramcontent.com/pod-product-compliance
Lightning Source LLC
Chambersburg PA
CBHW070106080526
44586CB00013B/1205